TO WAL

MULLETHEADS UNITE!

MULLETHEADS:

The Legends, Lore, Magic, and Mania
Surrounding the Humble but Celebrated Mullet

Michael Swindle

CRANE HILL
PUBLISHERS

Photograph on page 1 reprinted courtesy of UPI/Corbis-Bettmann.

The chapter titled "The Flora–Bama Interstate Mullet Toss" was originally published as "Mulletheads," in the May 13, 1997, issue of *The Village Voice.*

Published by Crane Hill Publishers, 3608 Clairmont Avenue, Birmingham, AL 35222; www.cranehill.com

Printed in the United States of America

Library of Congress Cataloging-in-Publication Data

Swindle, Michael, 1947-
Mulletheads: the legends, lore, magic, and mania surrounding the humble but celebrated mullet/Michael Swindle.
p.   cm.
ISBN 1-57587-074-6   ISBN 1-57587-084-3 (alk. paper)
1. Mullet—Humor. 2. Mullet fishing—Humor. I. Title.
PN6162.S94   1998
799.1'22—dc21   98-9438
                                                        CIP

10   9   8   7   6   5   4   3   2   1

This book is dedicated to my mother,

Juanita Colburn Swindle,

who despite her best efforts ended up
with a mullethead for a son anyway.

TABLE OF CONTENTS

ABOUT THE AUTHOR

Photograph by Linda Swindle

Michael Swindle was born in Birmingham, Alabama, in 1947 and now lives in New Orleans. His poetry has been published in numerous small press magazines, and his feature articles and reviews have appeared in many national publications, including *Details, The Village Voice, Inside Sports, Entertainment Weekly, Live! Magazine, The New York Times Book Review, The Washington Post, The Los Angeles Times,* and *Tattoo Advocate Journal.*

Mulletheads: The Legends, Lore, Magic, and Mania Surrounding the Humble but Celebrated Mullet is his first book-length work of nonfiction.

ACKNOWLEDGMENTS

I would like to express my sincere gratitude to the following people who offered me encouragement, support, assistance, kindness, and friendship as I traipsed up and down the Gulf Coast and then sat in my small office week after week after week trying to turn my travels into a book: Gordon Beene for planting the seed; Ellen Sullivan, of Crane Hill, without whom this project might never have gotten started; my editor, Norma McKittrick, without whose patient efforts this project might never have gotten finished; Barbara Barnes, of the Flora–Bama Lounge, for her good humor and the free beer; my sister, Nancy, and her husband, Michael McMullan, who turned me on to Dave "Mullet" Martin, who turned me on to Winston Luzier, who turned me on to Guy Asbury, at Siesta Fish Market; Maresa Pryor, for the great home cooking; the Spence family of Niceville, Florida—and especially Walt Spence, the "Voice of the Boggy Bayou Mullet Festival," for always being there when I needed guidance; James Campbell and the Boggy Boys Sportsman Club for simply being themselves; Grif Griffin for turning me on to Ted Peters Famous Smoked Fish; Michael Lathop for his keen insights and a lot of laughs; Bill Wilson, of the Barefoot Bar in Gulf Shores, for his colorful way with words; Randy Shutt, of Safe Harbor Seafood, who answered more questions than he really wanted to; Reggie Smith for taking me to work with him; *mi hermano* Alabama Billy Caldwell for his hospitality and wisdom—I still owe you for some long-distance calls; and most importantly, thanks beyond words to my wife, Linda, whose support on every level was unflagging and indispensable.

MULLETHEADS

Before mulletheads Jim and Sandy Schmidt moved from New Jersey to Florida four years ago, they didn't even know what a mullet was. Now every weekend they tow their Mullet Hut to the parking lot of Sunnybrook Shopping Plaza in Homosassa and serve up their homemade smoked mullet and smoked mullet spread. Photograph by Linda Swindle.

GENESIS: LA CASA DEL RIO

Many people, including my wife of twenty years, have asked me where my obsession with mullet came from. It is not an easy question to answer.

It makes me think of a couple I met, Jim Schmidt and his wife, Sandy, who moved from New Jersey to Homosassa, Florida, four years ago. They didn't know what a mullet was when they arrived down South, but now every weekend they tow a trailer that looks like a train caboose to the parking lot of Sunnybrook Shopping Plaza on Highway 19 and sell mullet that Jim catches and smokes himself.

"How did a guy from New Jersey," I asked Jim, "turn into a mullethead?"

He looked at me funny, and I knew he was registering the word "mullethead" the way most people do—as someone who is slow-witted. So I explained that I was using the term as a description of people whose lives are caught up with mullet in a serious way—like the Deadheads who used to follow the Grateful Dead around all over the world, like Jimmy Buffet fans calling themselves Parrotheads.

"I hadn't thought of it that way," Jim said, breaking into a grin, "but I guess I am a mullethead. I don't really know exactly how I came to be one though. It just happened."

It "just happened" to me also. I knew what a mullet was, of course, having seen them jumping in the water on rare occasions when I was on the water they were jumping in. But they held no special fascination for me until one evening in the spring of 1997 at La Casa del Rio.

La Casa is located on a small, secluded peninsula near the coast of Alabama, around which curls the Bon Secour River. It is owned by my friend Alabama Billy Caldwell, a kind and generous and totally wild soul who enjoys the benefit of being a real person and a fictional character in one of Barry Gifford's novels. (He sells a teenaged Sailor Ripley a banana-hued 1958 Buick Limited in *Baby Cat-Face.)*

Although Alabama Billy C built La Casa as a getaway spot for himself, it has become, over the years, a way station and retreat for a varied group of pilgrims belonging to the race of men described in the early years of this century by the vagabond poet laureate of Alaska, Robert Service, as those "who don't fit in." Some of the restless have proven worthy enough to hold keys to the compound at all times, others petition for access on an as-needed basis, and still others simply show up if the front gate is open. You never know who will turn up there, but it has been my experience that though the pilgrims who pass through may not fit in with society at large they fit in with each other.

One custom ritually observed at La Casa is that during daylight hours those in residence respect each other's privacy, everyone attending to his own business. (Unless there is monkey business afoot, in which case all assembled throw themselves into it with gusto.) Another custom, just as ritually observed, is a long and robust cocktail hour followed by a communally prepared meal followed by post-prandial libations (limited only by the constitutions of those participating) and conversation that is always lively and sometimes profound.

On the evening in question I found myself sharing Alabama Billy C's in absentia hospitality with a jolly fellow named Gordon. We had not met before, but as I have indicated that was not an unusual occurrence at La Casa.

If there was a reason for my being in that neck of the woods at the time, I have long forgotten it. But Gordon was in the area to indulge his newest passion: surf fishing. A subject about which I knew nothing.

Truth be told my father had cured me of hunting and fishing by the time I had reached my teens. Looking back on the brief time I spent at these activities in the wilds of hill country Mississippi, it was more like a week of Marine Corps training at Parris Island packed into one day—a quail hunt was a forced march beginning before sunrise and ending past sunset, the more briers to wade through the better; sitting in a fishing boat on a lake or river, waiting and waiting and waiting for the bite that never came was like being on an amphibious ambush, requiring an enforced silence and a sense of optimism that were simply alien to my basic nature. The man was serious, I'm telling you, serious about his hunting and fishing. And I just broke under the strain. I couldn't take it, so I turned to other activities.

But that was my problem, not Gordon's. He wanted, like all fresh converts, to talk about surf fishing. It being the shank of the night and my constitution holding up well, I thought I would begin at the beginning, so I asked him what he used for bait.

"Mullet," he said.

"That crazy jumping fish?"

"The very same."

"And where do you get these mullet?"

"I used to buy them at Delchamp's grocery," Gordon told me, "but I made a very important discovery just this morning. At the store they sell mullet for $1.98 a pound, which means one costs me two bucks. But today I found this fish house just downriver from here that will sell me a nice big mullet for a dollar."

"And how many mullet would a man need for a day of surf fishing?"

"One meets my needs," he replied. "I cut it into four chunks, and that will get me through as much fishing as I care to do in one day."

"But they eat mullet, don't they?"

"Absolutely. It's a little oily, and it has some dark meat along the blood line, but it's a delicious fish."

Then Gordon told me something that really caught my interest.

"They throw mullet too."

"Throw them?"

"Oh yeah. Every year the Flora–Bama Lounge has a big mullet toss where people sign up to see who can throw a mullet the farthest. It's coming up in a couple of weeks. You ought to check it out."

Yes, I thought to myself, that is a must.

What I had no inkling of at the time, however, was that out of this rather innocuous conversation would come months of ranging the sandy fields and roving the floods of the Gulf Coast, called to this gypsy roam by the siren song of the mullet but drawn on and on by the songs of the mulletheads I met along the way.

MULLET 101

Being somewhat at loose ends, I stayed on at La Casa del Rio after Gordon's departure, meditating on my immediate future as it were. Mulling things over, you could say. And as luck would have it, my host and benefactor and old pal Alabama Billy Caldwell appeared on the scene, unexpectedly, to help me clarify my thoughts.

After giving me a detailed account of his recent peregrinations—an overland driving trip from Birmingham to Belize—he inquired as to what it was I was up to.

"I've been pondering a writing project," I told him, "about mullet."

"Mullet, is it?" he said. "Well what do you know about them?"

"Hardly a thing," I responded.

"Good. Very good! It's an educational adventure then that you're after."

Billy had left home—and the American school system—at fifteen, and by his account has been in every country there is except Bali, Norway, Finland, mainland China, and the various regions of the former USSR, discounting the city of Moscow, where he once spent a few days admiring the subway system ("like museums!") and the vodka ("makes the expensive brands we get in this country taste like turpentine!"). Being an autodidact himself, he encourages self-improvement in others.

He disappeared into the library at La Casa, returned with an armload of books, and set them on the table at which I was sitting.

"This ought to get you started," he said.

● ● ● ● ●

The literature on mullet is not what you could call vast. By far the most instructive volume I consulted was *McClane's New Standard Fishing Encyclopedia and International Angling Guide* (henceforth referred to as *McClane's*), a weighty tome in terms of information and, at a little over 5 pounds, in heft as well. The following is, in synopsis, what I gleaned about mullet from the library at La Casa.

Mullet belong to the family Mugilidae (suckers, loosely translating the Latin). They are found in tropical and temperate marine waters throughout the world but will also travel in brackish and fresh water. There are 100 species of these small schooling fishes, including the European thin-lipped gray mullet and the European thick-lipped gray mullet; the freshwater mullet found in the coastal rivers of Australia; the white mullet, which swim the Atlantic Coast from Cape Cod to South America and along the Pacific Coast from Mexico to Chile; the golden-gray mullet of the Mediterranean; and the mullet called *ama'ama* in Hawaii, which are raised in ponds as a food source. The Basque word for mullet is *korkon*. They are called *bottarga* in Italy, *botargo* in Africa, and *batrakh* in the Middle East. The Finns know both the freshwater and saltwater varieties as *harjus* and love to eat them smoked.

There is a fish known as the red mullet, which is considered a delicacy in France and is a basic ingredient in bouillabaisse.

But it is really a member of the goatfish family, and not a mullet at all.

However the mullet on which we will focus our attention here is the striped mullet, *mugilidae cephalus,* "sucker head." This species is the most widely distributed geographically of the mullet family, found along both sides of the Atlantic and Pacific Oceans and in the Indian Ocean. But nowhere are they more plentiful than along the Florida and Alabama Gulf Coast where they are a local delicacy, most often eaten deep-fried or smoked. They are bottom feeders and for the most part vegetarians. Structurally they are akin to the barracuda, but they are at the opposite end of the scale as to ferociousness.

The striped mullet is a peculiar fish, and not only for its ability to live in salt, brackish, or fresh water. For one thing it is also known as the black mullet. For another this mullet has a gizzard—a muscular chamber in the alimentary canal, mostly found in birds and chickens, that grinds food. (Along the Gulf Coast, people will tell you that the mullet is the only fish with a gizzard, but there is a species of shad that also has one.)

In the 1920s three men who were arrested for fishing mullet out of season had the good sense—or the good luck—to hire a Tampa lawyer named Pat Whitaker. In his defense Whitaker put a biologist on the stand who testified that only birds have gizzards. The attorney then argued that his clients were innocent: Since mullet indisputably had gizzards, they were birds, not fish. The fishermen were found not guilty of the charges, and Whitaker later became president of the Florida state senate.

The central peculiar characteristic of mullet is their leaping ability. Unlike most leaping fish that jump from the water and reenter headfirst, the mullet leaps and holds its rigid posture, flopping back into the water on its belly or side. Often they make several leaps in a row.

Also, a whole school of mullet will leap together, slapping their tails on the water in what is called a "shower." Nobody really knows why they do this, but the most prominent scientific theory for this unusual behavior is that the mullet does it for the sheer joy of doing it.

● ● ● ● ●

No matter what type water they are living in, striped mullet head for saltwater when it is time for them to spawn. The spawning season, commonly called the roe season or the roe run, begins in mid-October and ends just after Christmas.

There are two kinds of roe. White roe, sometimes called "milt," is really the sperm of the male mullet. I never tried it, but people say if you coat it with cornmeal and flour and fry it to a golden brown, it tastes like oysters.

More popular by far is the female roe, called both red roe and yellow roe—red because the eggs are contained in a reddish membranous sac, and yellow because the thousands of tiny eggs inside the sac are like a fine, yellow paste. Red roe, smoked or fried and served with scrambled eggs, has long been a Cracker delicacy. The vast majority of the red roe harvested each year, however, is sold to the Japanese, who salt it and dry it for a dish called *karasumi,* which is traditionally served as a New Year's treat.

The female roe, which resembles a sausage when cooked, is delicate and rich and delicious. The only hazard is that if you eat too much of the roe, it can have a quick and unfailing laxative effect. ("Never trust a roe fart," one old-timer advised me.)

●   ●   ●   ●   ●

People will tell you that you have to use a net to catch mullet because they will not strike a baited hook. The truth of the matter is that mullet are not normally caught using a hook and line, but they can be, and have been, taken in this manner.

They can be finicky, however. *McClane's* notes one freshwater mountain mullet in Jamaica that prefers small pieces of avocado pear, and another variety called a calopeva that can only be caught using pieces of the local river moss that constitutes its regular diet.

As for our friend, the striped mullet of the Gulf Coast, several people volunteered stories of catching mullet with a hook and line. One afternoon at the Barefoot Bar in Gulf Shores, a well-to-do middle-aged lady, who from appearances would not be taken for a mullethead, effusively told me about hooking mullet from her dock on Mobile Bay. Her method was to scatter rabbit food on the water (it's called "chumming" in angler's parlance) to attract mullet, and then she would bait her hook with a single, small pellet of the rabbit food and catch mullet. It was, she insisted, a wonderful way to spend a morning or afternoon.

Morris Pate, of Plant City, Florida, remembered catching mullet as a child by chumming the water with crumbled bread and baiting his hook with a small bread ball. Jim Schmidt, in Homosassa, used something called cottonseed meal to chum the water and as bait. And Alabama Billy Caldwell swore he caught mullet when he was a youngster at Point Clear on the coast by using canned Green Giant Niblet Corn.

One of the most curious tales in this vein was told to me by eighty-six-year old Ted Peters, a raconteur of the first order and co-owner of one of the oldest smoked-mullet restaurants in Florida. "We had a fishing cooperative right after World War II, and the workers were cleaning grouper one day during the spawning season. Back in those days we just threw the entrails off the dock. Well the mullet got to feeding on that chum. My wife was there at the dock, and she got a hook and line and would put a little bit of gut on there, and she'd catch those mullet."

While it is true that mullet will bite a hook under the right circumstances or whenever they just want to, everyone who told me about trying to catch them that way also attested to the fact that it is not the ideal way to go. It is an activity that consumes a lot of time and is fraught with futility.

But, on second thought, these are not obstacles likely to deter a true mullethead.

● ● ● ● ●

It was curious to me as I traveled up and down the Gulf Coast to hear mullet talked about so often in what I call "cowboy" terms. Fishermen would describe fish they "herded out" of a certain area and talk about "roping on" so many pounds of mullet with their nets. One spoke of driving "the little dogies" up a draw and of the price he got for his fish "on the hoof." When two or more boats would strike their nets on a school of mullet, it was referred to as "circling the wagons." The historical marker in Cortez noted an early "fishing rancho" near the present site of the town.

These metaphors made a little more sense to me after reading a newspaper article in which mullet were called the "cattle of the ocean." They do indeed move about in large schools, or "herds," and like cattle they are placid vegetarians, "grazing" on algae and sea grasses.

Still it was amusing to me that mullet fishermen had themselves confused with cowboys.

"It's actually the other way around," Walt Spence, of the Boggy Bayou Mullet Festival, told me when I mentioned this to him. He went on to explain that Florida good old boys—rednecks in other parts of the South—are called "Crackers" and the term comes from the earliest settlers in the state who raised cattle and were always "cracking" their bullwhips as they worked their herds.

"So you see," he said, "it's cowboys who have confused themselves with fishermen."

●　●　●　●　●

The mullet is an unjustly maligned creature. It is a common thing to hear people refer to them as a "trash fish." Those doing the referring, I'm afraid, are either Yankees or stuck-up Southerners. Certainly they are the victims of misinformation and their own ignorance. And most certainly they have never eaten a mullet.

Part of the problem probably stems from the fact that mullet are bottom feeders. This reality seems to really bother some people, but the salient point is that they feed on sea grasses and other plant life. They are not scavengers like crabs, which will eat any kind of decaying flesh including that of humans if given the opportunity, and only a fool would refuse to eat crabmeat.

Mullet are at their best when fresh, and since they don't "travel well," mulletheads must follow Mohammed's example and "go to" the mullet. Photograph by Winston Luzier.

Mullet is invariably, to my great delight, described as having a "nutty" flavor, and that is an apt description on two levels. But in dealing with mullet you have a "Mohammed and the mountain" situation. Just as the mountain would not come to Mohammed, the mullet will not come to you. They do not travel well. Mullet can be frozen but only for short periods of time. They are at their best when they are fresh so that means you must go to the mullet.

That's what I did, and I have not regretted it for one moment.

WHAT'S IN A NAME?

I stopped in one afternoon to talk to Ike Thomas, proprietor of My–Way Seafood in Panacea, Florida. "I'm writing a book about mullets," I told him as an introduction.

His quick rejoinder was, "You writing a book about the different kinds of mullet or one about the mullet we catch around here?"

He had me there, and I relate this as a cautionary tale so that mullet-deficient readers who may wish to explore the world of mullet and mulletheads won't make the same mistake.

Along the Gulf Coast the word "mullet" is both a singular and a plural noun, like the word "deer." This is fairly common in the fish world—the same holds true for trout, for instance, or for grouper or bass (nobody talks about catching a mess of "basses"). So be forewarned—don't stand out as a greenhorn by saying things like "I caught some mullets" or "I'd like a plate of mullets."

In Spanish mullet is (or are, you could say) called "lisa" (a factoid that several of my women friends who bear that name were none too happy about my discovering). Back in the 1960s the State of Florida felt the fish known as "mullet" was so wrongly maligned so strongly in the minds of the noncognoscenti—i.e., it could not shake its reputation as a "trash fish"—that they decided to officially change its name. A canned product under the name "Lisa" was produced and marketed, but it didn't pan out.

Naturally people being asked to buy the product wanted to know what "lisa" was. Upon finding out that it was mullet, they might as well have been told it was "roadkill." That was the end of that experiment, and now about your only chance of hearing a mullet called a lisa is if you're baiting a hook while sportfishing in Mexico or Costa Rica.

Francis Spence, founder of the Boggy Bayou Mullet Festival in Niceville, Florida, once had the idea of canning smoked mullet and marketing it under the brand name "Boggy Bacon." Being a man of limited recklessness, however, he took a lesson from the "Lisa" fiasco and shelved his plan.

A more successful name change was orchestrated by my friend Bill Wilson at the Barefoot Bar in Gulf Shores. "I used to make a smoked mullet spread," he told me, "and I sold it for $3.95. It was mighty tasty, but people just weren't ordering it. Well it came time to print some new menus, and I called it 'fish pate,' upped the price to $5.95, and couldn't make enough of the stuff!"

RUSTY'S

I didn't know if I liked mullet or not when Alabama Billy Caldwell took me to Rusty's Restaurant and Lounge located on Grand Lagoon between Pensacola and the Florida–Alabama state line. Some years ago I had ordered mullet at a place down here, but the party I was with included a number of criminal defense attorneys, and much spirituous liquor was ordered and consumed. I either ate my mullet and don't remember doing so, or I forgot to eat it altogether.

That makes Rusty's the official site of my first mess of fried mullet. And lo, it was good, very good. As with first love, this laid-back haven for mulletheads will always have a special place in my heart.

Rusty's used to be called Rusty's Rendezvous (named for a family cousin), and it used to be across the narrow shell road from the present site, right on the water. Like most enterprises entered into by mulletheads, it was not so much planned as it just happened. Leo Roszak came south from Chicago in the 1950s and bought a boat launch and fish camp. No heavy lifting was involved, and that suited Leo fine. He could kick back, have a beer or two, and listen to fish tales, pretty much what Florida Crackers have been doing for over a hundred years.

In 1960 Leo married a local girl, Dannie Lokey, who decided to spruce up the kitchen at the fish camp. This caught the notice of the mullet fishermen who used the boat launch, and they began asking her to fry up some of their catch at the end of the day. She was happy to oblige so long as her Uncle Joe cleaned the fish.

Fried mullet is fine, but it is certainly enhanced by a pile of hush puppies and creamy coleslaw. Dannie started whipping up this combination and served it all in aluminum dishpans so everybody could help themselves. In short order Rusty's Rendezvoux was doing a thriving business in all-you-can-eat fried mullet "dishpan style."

On September 12, 1979, the business literally came crashing down when Hurricane Frederick flattened this stretch of the Gulf Coast.

That would be the end of the story for Rusty's except for the efforts of Paul Feran and wife, Louella, who is Dannie's daughter. Seven years to the day after the destruction of Hurricane Frederick, on September 12, 1986, the Ferans with their daughter, Beth, and son, John Edward, opened a rebuilt Rusty's.

By Memorial Day weekend 1989 they had created a full-service restaurant in a rambling tri-level country-style house overlooking Grand Lagoon. Captain Feran had served in the navy as a light attack pilot and in his last assignment as captain of the aircraft carrier U.S.S. *Lexington*. A raised 01-L lounge ("oh-one level" is naval jargon for the first level above the main deck of a ship) was added on to the original dining room, and at another level beyond that the alfresco "topside" bar. All of this now presided over by the "real" owners: about three dozen cats that wander and sleep where they choose.

When the Ferans reopened Rusty's they brought back

One night while Captain Feran was cleaning the day's catch of mullet, a customer asked him to fry up the backbones for him. He did—and Rusty's has been selling this mullet delicacy ever since.

"dishpan style" mullet, but the rapacious, let's-get-over attitude that began in the 1980s put an end to that tradition.

"There's a different type customer now," Captain Feran says. "We used to have a regular metal dishpan and we'd put everything in there—your steak fries, hush puppies, mullet, sometimes even your coleslaw. But then we'd find that four guys would come in and order one grilled cheese sandwich and an all-u-can-eat mullet dinner. First thing you know we've got twenty-two mullet going up there and this one guy is supposedly eating them all. We never used to have that problem in the old days. Now that's the type of thing you have to deal with. We actually stopped serving in the dishpans before the net ban."

Feran and his son had a mullet boat for a while, and using an 1,100-foot gill net 18 feet deep they would go out and "round up" fish for the restaurant. That activity ended when the gill net was banned in Florida in 1995.

Everyone involved with mullet has his own take on the net ban, and Captain Feran is no exception. "This restaurant used to cook about 1,500 pounds of mullet a week," he says. "Then a fellow from Taiwan came by and asked me who my wholesaler was, and I told him. Well he started mobilizing everybody. Started buying roe during roe season. The Japanese would pay about thirty bucks a pound for the roe, which meant the wholesalers around here were getting about twelve bucks. And the first thing you know during roe season all the wholesalers were slaughtering thousands and thousands of pounds of mullet a day and throwing the carcasses away. Then a funny thing happened. We started getting fewer and fewer mullet. And no one knew why. Abortions were really working!

"The commercial fishing industry didn't want any controls at all," he continued. "The sportfishermen wanted very strict controls. Mullet is the rabbit of the ocean, and all the other fish feed on it too—they tried and tried to get restrictive bills passed. Finally the state legislature passed a bill, but the governor, rumor had it, got the biggest bribe of his career and he pocket-vetoed the bill.

"That infuriated all the sportfishing clubs so they went out and got 750,000 signatures on a petition that called for a referendum to change the constitution of the State of Florida banning use of the traditional gill net. The referendum passed, and that put us where we are now."

No matter whose side you're on—the commercial fishermen or the sportfishermen—there are fewer mullet on the market these days as a result of the net ban. That means the price is up. Captain Feran remembers mullet costing sixteen cents a pound in the 1960s, cleaned, dressed, iced down, and delivered to you. Before 1995 he was paying fifty cents a pound. Now he pays $1.29 a pound or more, and he gets his mullet from Alabama, where the gill net is still legal.

Back in the "old days" serving mullet was pretty simple too. You'd take off the heads, of course, and the scales, gut it, and then fry it in peanut oil. Nobody filleted mullet. "Have you seen the locals eat the whole mullet?" asks Captain Feran. "First they eat the tails, like potato chips, and by the time they get through with it, it looks like a cat's been at it."

That has changed a little in recent days though. Folks on this neck of the coast still like their mullet fried, the way they've been eating it for generations. But increasingly they want such niceties as fillets and finger fillets, rather than a whole fried mullet.

The counterbalance to this newfound sophistication is the undisputed delicacy of the house: fried mullet backbones, or "Cracker popsicles" as they are known in some circles.

"I was cleaning mullet one night," Captain Feran says, "and I usually throw the backbones aside to use for bait in crab traps. This friend of mine was in here, and he says, 'Don't throw those away. Fry them up for me.' Well he ate them, and when he got up to leave, he threw a couple bucks on the table. I asked what that was for, and he said for the backbones. Another guy sitting there said, 'Let me try some of those.'

"You know that old saying, the closer to the bone, the sweeter the meat? Well that's true with fish too. People strip them down and eat them with beer. Hell, now I get $3.25 for six backbones as an appetizer. Add some beans, slaw, and steak fries, and you have a dinner for $5.95—for something I used to throw away."

Contestants in the annual Flora–Bama Interstate Mullet Toss throw footlong (yes, they are dead) mullets from the Florida side of the state line down a 50-foot-wide 200-foot-long "alley" into Alabama. Photograph by Bryce Lankard.

THE FLORA–BAMA INTERSTATE MULLET TOSS

John from Odenville, Alabama, was mugging for the camera, arms spread, a mullet stuffed headfirst into his mouth.

This was my introduction to the 13th Annual Interstate Mullet Toss at the legendary Flora–Bama Lounge, which sits astride the Alabama–Florida state line. The Flora–Bama opened in 1962 as a small roadhouse and package store, but it is now a honky-tonk empire, open 365 days a year, that consists of a 100-foot beachfront, three live-music stages, an oyster bar, a limousine service, a recording studio, and ten—count 'em, ten!—full-service bars.

Lightning crackled out over the Gulf of Mexico, thunder rolled in with the waves, and tropical rain beat down steadily. It did not seem to me a propitious day for the throwing of mullet.

John from Odenville, however, set me straight, exclaiming to anyone within earshot, "When you throwing mullet, dammit, it's rain or shine!"

● ● ● ● ●

Thirteen years ago Flora–Bama owner Joe Gilchrist was trying to come up with an idea to beef up his business in the early spring. His friend Jimmy Louis, a musician and songwriter, suggested a contest in which people would compete to see how far they could toss a mullet from Florida into Alabama. Gilchrist, a laid-back sort of guy, thought, "Why not?"

From this simple and wacky start, the Mullet Toss has turned into an annual festival that draws more than 60,000 people over three days. Most come simply to party, but almost 1,200 people sign up for the Mullet Toss.

Why do they do it? I don't know. The mullet is said to possess mystical properties. I repeat this exactly as it was presented to me, without further elaboration or explanation. I just don't know. The phenomenon is simply ineffable. Put out a barrel of mullet, and someone will come to throw one.

●　●　●　●　●

Mullet used in the Toss weigh approximately a pound and are a little over a foot long. (And in answer to the single-most-often asked question I get when telling people about mullet tossing: Yes, they are dead.) They are tossed from a 10-foot throwing circle on the Florida side of the state line down a 50-foot-wide rectangular "alley" that stretches 200 feet into Alabama. The sideline boundaries and 25-foot sections the length of the alley are marked off with orange tape.

"We are burdened with so many rules in this life," Joe Gilchrist explained to me, "mostly by the government, that we try to keep them to a minimum at the Toss."

The rules are indeed few and reasonable. You may kiss your mullet, but you cannot pour beer into it. If you step out of the throwing circle during your throw or follow-through, you are disqualified, and the same goes for throwing your fish out of bounds. You can't use gloves. The mullet must be sand free. And you must retrieve your own mullet and deposit it in the designated water bucket (the mullet are recycled). You get only one qualifying throw.

Whether you throw your mullet overhand, underhand, sidearm, discus, football, baseball, or meatball style, you get only one qualifying throw. Photograph by Bryce Lankard.

There are several tossing styles. One can grasp the mullet by the tail and toss it either overhand, underhand, or sidearm. (This style is looked down upon by veteran tossers because, they say, the mullet will slip too easily out of your hand.) There is the football-style toss, which is self-explanatory. Joe Gilchrist demonstrated his "airplane" technique of tossing, explaining how you must adjust the side fins just so to get proper aerodynamics, etcetera, but I don't think any serious tosser would put much faith in this method.

John from Odenville, who was making his maiden toss, had an interesting tossing style, holding the mullet by its tail, spinning like a discus thrower, and releasing in the middle of the third spin. I wouldn't recommend this method. It looked good, but John didn't make the cut.

Far and away the most popular and most effective tossing style was the "baseball" or "meatball" style. The mullet is folded (as nearly as is possible) in half, with the tail on top, gripped with the fingers with head forward and held firmly with the thumb. The release is as if you were throwing a baseball in from deep center field.

Qualifying takes place over two days, and the six contestants in each category recording the longest distances meet in the championship finals. There are fifteen categories in the competition for men and women, grouped by age, from ages one through seven to seventy-plus.

Mullet tossing, however, is a young man's game. Most of the attention is on the twenty-one through thirty-nine-year-old men's division, where the longest distances are attained and the records are set.

The record distance in the Mullet Toss is 178 feet and is held by twenty-six-year-old Michael "Woody" Bruhn, a fire-protection system installer from Spring Hill, Tennessee, a small town south of Nashville. Woody (his nickname comes from the fact that he is the spitting image of the actor Woody Harrelson) not only holds the world record for mullet

Woody Bruhn demonstrates his award-winning grip on a mullet. He holds the world record for mullet tossing: 178 feet. Photograph by Bryce Lankard.

tossing, but also he has been the champion of the Mullet Toss for the past three years.

"I really can't say in so many words," Woody told me when I asked what had drawn him to mullet tossing. "I was down here five years ago on vacation. I didn't throw that year, but I saw all the pictures of the Mullet Toss on the Flora–Bama's walls, and when I got back home I just decided I had to have my picture up there too. So I've been here every year since and been lucky enough to have won the thing three years in a row. It just came naturally to me."

Woody, of course, uses the baseball tossing method, but he does no special training other than "just drink a few beers and keep my arm loose."

In his qualifying throw on Saturday, Woody showed he was the man to beat, with a distance of 178 feet 3 inches.

•　　•　　•　　•　　•

On Sunday the weather cleared, and a huge crowd was on hand for the finals. I found Woody watching the last of the qualifiers, sipping a beer.

"They say there's a guy out here with a pretty good arm," he told me, "but I haven't seen him throw yet."

Not that he seemed worried, but I pointed out nobody had tossed anywhere near his 178 feet 3 inches.

"I won't throw that far today," Woody said. "There's no rain, but the wind is way stronger than yesterday."

The three finalists up before Woody tossed 98 feet, 127 feet 8 inches, and 123 feet, respectively. Woody positioned his mullet to his satisfaction and windmilled his throwing arm a few times. He got off a fine toss, but at 146 feet 6 inches, it was not up to his championship record form.

He was, however, now four-time Champion of the Interstate Mullet Toss, and we chatted briefly as he collected his prizes: a hand-painted mullet plaque, a big plastic Miller Lite battery-operated wall clock, and a $50 bar tab at the Flora–Bama.

"I don't think I'm gonna toss next year," Woody confided to me as he accepted congratulations from his peers.

"Why not?" I asked.

"When you're in competition," he said, with a big *Cheers*-y grin, "you have to stay too sober."

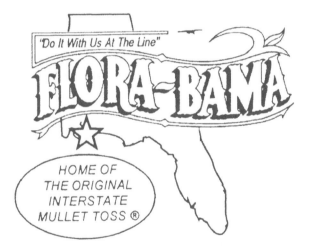

IN MULLET

WE TRUST

MULLET TOSSING
IN MONTGOMERY

Dave "Mullet" Martin—he was given the nickname years ago by his roommate at the University of Florida—is an Associated Press photographer in Montgomery, Alabama. His story is not an especially pretty one, but like the tale of Gilgamesh it is worth retelling.

Montgomery is the state capital, but unless the legislature is in session it is the kind of small town where you have to make your own entertainment. Townsfolk tend to throw a lot of parties, and Dave and his wife are no exception. Their "annual" party was inaugurated in 1987. Sometimes it would be in the winter, sometimes in the summer—whenever the party spirit moved them.

Because Dave was proud of his nickname, he called the party his Annual Mullet Festival. He always provided a supply of smoked mullet (the only way to cook it as far as he is concerned), and the evening always included a mullet toss that his guests could participate in if they wished.

He printed up rather elaborate and humorous T-shirts for the party. One year he had two Irish setters holding mullet in their mouths on the front, and on the back, "Don't Shake That Mullet In My Face." The front logo of another said "High Plains Mullet," with a mullet dressed like Clint Eastwood holding an Uzi, and the back said "Welcome to Mullet Hell." Still another had "Man & Mullet" on the front, picturing a mullet holding a small man in its fin, and on the back, "Another romp in the wrong direction down the evolutionary path."

The party was very popular, and it was not unusual for the affair to draw 300 people over the course of the evening. Fellow newspaper people would fly in from as far away as Manhattan and Mexico City.

Everything went swimmingly until one night in 1992. There had been nothing out of the ordinary really. At least not for one of Dave's parties. People had eaten their fill of smoked mullet. The mullet toss, as always, had commenced at the stroke of midnight. Rules for the toss, as they invariably are, were simple: You had to stay behind the throwing line— a crack in the pavement in front of Dave's house—when you let go of your mullet and you had to retrieve your own fish.

Things had pretty much wound down, actually, when the police, responding to an anonymous complaint, arrived at 2:30 in the morning. They told Dave they had been sitting in their patrol car two blocks away where they could hear loud noise, and they had observed people "throwing dead fish." Dave maintains to this day that no one had thrown a mullet for well over an hour by the time the police showed up. Most people liked to toss early because the mullet were recycled and weren't in very good shape after hitting the pavement a few times. He did admit, though, that a good toss elicited a pretty loud response from the assembled party-goers.

The police, however, carted Dave off to jail on a charge of disturbing the peace, which transmuted into something called "creating prohibitive noise" by the time his brother-in-law bailed him out five hours later. "As we walked out of the city jail," Dave remembers, "the police car that had brought me in was sitting in the parking lot. As we got closer to it, I had to crack up. I assume it had been on patrol the whole time I was in lockup, surely bringing in more arrested people, but wedged between the sideview mirror and the car door was a lonely, reeking mullet somebody at the party had stuffed in there."

Going to jail had not been funny, but Dave had one last, and very long, laugh that foggy Sunday morning. As his brother-in-law turned his car onto Dave's street, all they could see in the low beams of the headlights were the shining eyes of about two dozen cats looking up at them from the mullet they were feasting on.

A young mullethead shows off his championship form at the Lillian Mullet Festival. Photograph courtesy of The Onlooker.

THE LILLIAN MULLET FESTIVAL

It was the Sunday night before Labor Day, and I was ensconced back at La Casa del Rio enjoying a solitary and peaceful respite after spending the day at the 10th Anniversary Annual Mullet Festival in Lillian, a beautiful little unincorporated town on the Alabama border, just before the bridge that takes you over the north end of Perdido Bay into Florida.

I might have missed this festival if I had not been in a hurry back in August to get over to Pensacola to check out some mullet restaurants. Instead of taking the scenic beach drive from La Casa del Rio through Gulf Shores, I drove up to Foley and took Highway 98 East, a much faster route. As I rolled through Lillian, what did I spy but a sign on the side of the road announcing the festival. Ah, serendipity! Seek and ye shall find (or bump into when ye are not really looking). There is no such thing as a coincidence!

Sponsored by the Optimist Club of Perdido Bay to raise money for various area youth groups, the festival is held at the Lillian Community Club and draws nearly 2,000 people over the weekend. There are clowns, games, and train and pony rides for the kids; a bake sale; food and beer; a turkey shoot; souvenir T-shirts; arts and crafts; bands and singers and cloggers; a dunk tank; a $5,000 raffle, with the winning ticket delivered from 13,000 feet by skydivers; and, as the saying goes, much, much more.

Naturally the mullet dinner is the highlight of the food offerings: "deliciously fried mullet, coated with yellow and white cornmeal, served with breaded okra, hush puppies, salad, potatoes, bread, coffee/tea, and dessert." For a mere six bucks, you just can't beat it!

Anyway, I'd had my mullet dinner and was back at La Casa nursing a rather stronger beverage than had been available to me in Lillian and taking a look at the festival activities for Labor Day as listed in the local paper, *The Islander*. There was a 7:30 a.m. breakfast (skip it), a 5K "Run for the Mullet" (skip it), and what was called a "Mullet Fling" (whoa!).

As reported, "Tony Kichler went into the record book last year with a fling of 151 feet 6 inches. Ricky Waltman was second in last year's fling (135 feet 3 inches), and Rice Drummond was third (117 feet 10 inches)."

That winning fling was pretty respectable, but respectable or not, when mullet are being flung, a man wants to be present if he can. And I could.

As I sat quietly pondering the metaphysics of flinging mullet, there suddenly arose a clatter at the front door that turned out to be my old pal Morris Pate, whom I had not seen in some time. After hearty *abrazos*, Morris explained that he had been in Birmingham for the opening game of the University of Alabama Crimson Tide's 1997 football season, a game in which the Tide had handily defeated the University of Houston, 42-17. He was on his way home to Plant City, Florida, and decided to lay over a night at La Casa, not knowing he would find me there.

I must point out here that Morris is a fanatic about Alabama football—the diminutive "fan" does not suffice. I am in that category also, along with thousands of others, not only in the state of Alabama, but across the nation and in far-flung places like Finland. Football in the South is a religion, and Saturday is the Holy Day. And please take my word for it, followers of Alabama are the most fervent of the lot.

So Morris was in extremely high spirits after the first win of the season. He treated me to an expensive meal, after which we returned to La Casa and talked into the wee hours. We covered a wide variety of topics, but primarily we focused on the past and future successes of the Crimson Tide.

You probably have foreseen the results of this reunion. I overslept. It was 9:30 when I cracked an eyelid to look at the bedside clock. In a frenzy I dressed and dashed downstairs, passing a groggy Morris coming from the kitchen with a cup of coffee.

"I gotta go," I yelled on the run. "I'm late!"

As I was pulling out of the carport, Morris was at the front door in his bathrobe, waving good-bye and bellowing, "ROLL TIDE!"

Normally the drive from La Casa in Bon Secour to Lillian takes about forty-five minutes tops. But it was Labor Day— end of vacation! When I got to the highway that takes you to Foley and Highway 98, the traffic leaving Gulf Shores was bumper to bumper. And not moving.

The short version is that it took me over two hours to get to the festival. Walking around the Lillian Community Club building toward the ball field, I passed by the lemonade booth run by Juanita and her husband, Milton, whom I'd met the day before.

"Michael," Juanita called out to me. "Where have you been? They've already thrown the mullets."

Damn.

I accepted a tall glass of lemonade from Juanita and found a folding chair under a nearby portable tent, the kind you find at this type event—and at funerals. Sipping the cold lemonade, the veins in my temples pounded rhythmically.

And the rhythm seemed to say, "You . . . have . . . found . . . the . . . mullet . . . head . . . with . . . in . . . your . . . self."

Craftier mullet escape fishing nets by simply leaping over the top and heading for freedom. Photograph by Winston Luzier.

MULLET WRAPPERS

Reggie Smith's day begins at 5:30 a.m. with breakfast and an extra cup of coffee with his first mate, Pat. There is a stop to gas up his truck and the fuel tanks on his boat, and then almost an hour's drive from the north end of Perdido Bay, just across the state line in Florida, to Safe Harbor Seafood, which backs up to the Bon Secour (pronounced Se-cure by locals) River, about a mile before it empties into Mobile Bay.

Safe Harbor (the English translation of Bon Secour) is run by John Shutt and his son, Randy. They have a small retail seafood market in the front section of the fish-cleaning house, but their main business is on the wholesale side. They sell anything that swims in the Gulf, but they are really "mullet kings," handling more of that species than anybody on the Alabama Coast and probably along the Florida Panhandle too.

Though I am not an early riser I arrived at Safe Harbor before Reggie and Pat—I did not want to take a chance on getting left behind. It had not been easy to get myself invited to go out with a commercial fisherman. I had no one to act as an intermediary for me, and Randy had been dubious when I approached him for assistance in meeting some mullet wrappers.

Alabama is the only state on the Gulf Coast that has not banned the controversial gill net, and mullet fishermen and fish dealers are sensitive to the fact that the legal tide could turn against them in a heartbeat. Therefore they are wary of outsiders, especially those professing to be writers.

It took me several visits to convince Randy that I was not a spy for a sportfishing organization. But I wore him down, and he introduced me to Reggie, who has been netting mullet for fourteen years, the greater part of his adult life. A tall, rangy, weather-beaten guy, full of good humor, Reggie agreed to take me along as an observer—so long as I bought the beer at the end of the day.

Reggie is one of a large number of mullet wrappers who contract with Safe Harbor to sell their catch. And the rule is, according to Reggie, "when the price of mullet goes up, it goes up a nickel a pound. When the price goes down, it always goes down ten cents a pound. Always. That's the way it works."

The fish house is the last stop before Reggie puts his boat in the water and begins the day's work. While Pat shovels a load of ice onto the boat, Reggie has another cup of coffee and talks mullet, weather, and luck with his fellow fishers.

Iced up, we drive out Fort Morgan Road to Mobile Bay, where Reggie puts the boat in at a small lagoon. There is a real marina and boat launch facility only a mile up the road, but the sportfishermen who use it convinced the owner to stop allowing gill netters to put in there.

"There's just a lot of animosity between the sportsmen and the commercials," Reggie says, "but the owner is really an OK guy. He lets us dock up there if a big storm blows in."

Reggie fishes out of a 26-foot fiberglass "kicker boat," a boat powered by an outboard motor, the "kicker"—in Reggie's case a 120-horsepower Johnson. There is a type of kicker boat, known as a "bow boat," that has the outboard motor mounted in the bow of the boat, leaving the stern free of obstructions so the fishermen can work their nets. Reggie however has his motor mounted on the starboard (right) side of the stern transom so the net can be thrown and pulled back in from the port side. The boat is steered from a raised captain's chair in the bow that allows Reggie to scout the water for schools of mullet. A large double-compartment fish box fills the midship, one side filled with crushed ice that is shoveled onto the fish in the other side to keep them fresh.

The net Reggie uses is 1,600 feet long with a depth of 14 feet. The net's mesh, the openings in the clear monofilament netting, is just under 3 inches. (During roe season, when the mullet are fatter, he will use a net with a 4-inch mesh.) The bottom line on which the net is hung, called the lead line, is weighted naturally enough with lead and carries the net to its full depth. The top line, the float line, is filled with something called Spongex that keeps the top of the net floating on the surface of the water.

Our first few hours on the water are spent "burning gas," cruising along the coastline or from one part of Mobile Bay to another, scouting for a black knot of schooled mullet, or bobbing in the water scouring the horizon for jumping mullet. The wind is not exactly right and neither is the tide, for reasons I do not understand but nod sagely upon hearing anyway.

One thing I grasp is that a single mullet jumping doesn't excite gill netters. It's what they call a "lonely" mullet, separated from the school and trying to rejoin his comrades. What they look for is several mullet rocketing out of the water. And just before noon that is what we find ourselves watching.

Then the action begins. It is time to strike the net.

"Throw it," Reggie shouts, and Pat tosses the "let-go," an inflatable orange buoy attached to the end of the net that anchors it in place. Reggie guns the motor, and the net runs out over the side of the boat in a wide circle around the school of mullet. He idles the motor so that Pat can tip the 120 Johnson forward out of the water, enabling the boat to glide over the float line of the net at the let-go end, closing the circle. Then he accelerates and wheels the boat in circles, running out the remainder of the net in an ever smaller spiral inside the initial rope-off until the net plays out. Wrapping the mullet in the net—mullet wrapping.

Some mullet ram the outside wall of the net headfirst, the mesh of the net holding them tight around their gills, cutting off their air supply. They are "gilled" in the mesh, which is how the net gets its name. Other mullet, sensing danger, break away from the outside wall of the net, only to ram into and stick to the inside net walls of the strike. If a mullet is large enough it can break through the mesh, but normally escape is effected only by the craftier of the mullet who simply leap over the float line and head for freedom.

Once the mullet are corralled, Reggie and Pat take a break to allow the free-swimming fish to "net up." The soundtrack for this scene consists of the thrashing of the mullet gilled in the net, the slash and plop of mullet leaping over the net, and the boisterous splash and settle of the inevitable brown pelicans arriving for an easy meal.

"Everybody's got to eat," Reggie says of the pelicans snapping at the gilled mullet and trying to gobble them free of the net.

One reason for his philosophical attitude is that the pelicans serve as guides for gill netters. A flock of circling pelicans dive-bombing a stretch of water to feed often signals the presence of a large school of mullet.

This short break over, the real work begins. The two men lean into pulling 1,600 feet of net back onto the boat. Reggie takes the float line (it's lighter and he's the captain after all), and Pat tugs on the lead line. Wearing cotton gloves they "shuck" gilled mullet from the net—grasping the fish firmly and pushing it headfirst through the net mesh and flipping it into the fish box, stopping now and then to shovel in a layer of ice.

They gauge the duration of this chore by how far they are from the floating orange let-go at the end of the net, and as they shuck the mullet they arrange the empty net on the deck of the boat in perfect position for their next strike.

We had a baseball kind of day as it turned out—three net strikes and we were out of the water. Reggie estimated the catch at 700 pounds, certainly more mullet than I had ever seen but only a so-so catch as far as Reggie and Pat were concerned.

"You should have been here two weeks ago," Reggie told me, exhibiting a trait particular to fishermen down through the ages. "We caught 14,000 pounds of mullet in ten days! Kind of got us spoiled."

The day's work over except for weighing the mullet at Safe Harbor and tallying the payment, we tore into some iced-down beer. It was Busch, which I can tell you with no hesitation after extensive scientific investigation up and down the coasts of Alabama and Florida, is the official beer of mulletheads. (Walt Spence, of Boggy Bayou, says it's simply the cheapest beer you can buy that anyone will still drink.)

"Well, I guess we got our share today," Reggie said, cracking number two. "Though I was hoping to get somebody else's share too."

BOGGY COUNTRY

I had never heard of Niceville, Florida, until I heard about the Boggy Bayou Mullet Festival, and I heard about that one August afternoon when I was in the French Quarter bending an elbow with Markie B., an Irish rapscallion of my acquaintance, whose love of the drink and high jinx in general belies a surprising erudition. How he knew about it is anybody's guess. The odd had become the norm ever since I started chasing mullet and mulletheads.

No matter the circumstances the fact that I discovered the festival and the town was one small and isolated vindication of the vision of Francis Spence, who dreamed up the idea of a mullet festival to bring attention to his Florida Panhandle hometown on the north shore of Choctawhatchee Bay, at the headwaters of Boggy Bayou.

The Spence family history goes back over a hundred years, from before the town even had a name, when the area was just a scattered settlement of maybe sixty people and was known simply as Boggy Bayou, or Old Boggy. Francis's grandfather, S. S. Spence ("the first S was for Sylvester, and the second wasn't for anything,"), was a prominent hog farmer and a member of the committee that was formed to come up with an official name for the town for the U.S. Postal Service. (It seems that some people who counted did not want their mail postmarked "Old Boggy, FL.")

The committee's first choice was Portsmouth, but that name was rejected because it was too similar to a town 21 miles away called Portland. Mr. B. R. Edge, who happened to be the post-master, had suggested the name Niceville, and it was the name officially assigned. Though most people still call the area Boggy Country.

In 1976 Francis Spence was the president of the local chamber of commerce, and his brainstorm was born of irritation. He would make business calls and announce himself and where he was calling from, and the voice at the other end of the line would ask, "You're Mr. Smith from Nashville?" He decided what the area needed was a seafood festival and that the centerpiece of the festival should be the mullet, "that feisty underdog amongst seafood," a fish that has always been an integral part of the local culture.

In the early days in Old Boggy, people worked at sawmilling and making turpentine, but mostly they made their living, and fed their families, from the waters of Choctawhatchee Bay, which runs 30 miles, east from Fort Walton to Point Washington, and measures 8 miles at its widest point. They harvested trout, flounder, shrimp, oysters, bass, bream, sturgeon, and of course lots and lots of mullet.

The Choctawhatchee was originally mostly a freshwater bay, fed by the Choctawhatchee River. In 1929, however, that would change forever. There was a bad flood in the spring of that year and the water in the bay rose about 10 feet. People over in Destin, directly across from Niceville on the south side of the bay, began to fear they would be flooded out. A fellow by the name of Odom Melvin had the bright idea that he would cut a little trench across his land in Destin that would allow the swollen bay water to run into the Gulf. He didn't consult with anyone, he just took a few men and some shovels and dug a trench about 60 feet long from the bay to the Gulf.

What he hadn't reckoned on was that the water in the Gulf was higher than the water in the bay. In less than an hour the Gulf water rushed into the bay, creating a new pass approximately 600 feet wide and 10 feet deep, and Mr. Melvin and his crew were lucky to escape with their lives.

Naturally the Choctawhatchee was turned into a saltwater bay, which killed all the freshwater fish and left . . . well lots and lots of mullet.

Around 1910 a man named Aaron Howell had two boats built that revolutionized mullet fishing in the Choctawhatchee. Called "bay boats," they resembled a houseboat, with a cabin that would sleep a crew of four and a large deck where mullet were salted down in barrels. Two skiffs were towed so the mullet were still netted in the traditional manner, but the bay boats allowed the fisherman to stay out for several days and work the entire length of the bay instead of their former range of 5 miles or so.

After World War II another revolution hit the mullet-fishing world: the outboard motor. Before the war outboard motors had been heavy and inefficient and costly to run, but by 1950 they were lighter, faster, and cheaper, so they displaced the old bay boats. Synthetic monofilament nets, which didn't have to be bleached and dried after every use, arrived on the scene around the same time to make life easier for the mullet fisherman.

And of course the latest and saddest chapter in the history of mullet fishing came to Niceville as well as the rest of Florida: the gill net ban. "A way of life had ended," as Francis Spence says, "after many generations."

● ● ● ● ●

I went to Niceville looking for mulletheads, and I found them aplenty. But they were already calling themselves "fishheads."

Jack C. Nichols, coauthor of *Up, Down, In & Around Boggy Bayou,* writes: "It was the nom de plume assigned to us by the soldiers stationed out at Eglin Field during the late thirties and early forties. The thing about it was they meant it to be a derogatory description of the local fishermen who walked the dusty streets of Old Boggy in cutoff dungarees without the benefit of shirt or shoes! In our way of thinking, we owed our survival in a large part to the bounties that the sea afforded us. Therefore we accepted the soldiers' designation with great pride and determination to defend it from dishonor."

The designation remains one of pride to natives of Niceville. It is "one that cannot be earned or adopted. It has to be a genetic transmission at birth."

● ● ● ● ●

The first Boggy Bayou Mullet Festival was a one-day event, held on Saturday, September 24, 1977, at White Point, a beach east of town. Some 35,000 people showed up, and there was no turning back. Now the festival is a three-day event, the third weekend in October, and consistently draws crowds of 150,000 and up.

Most of the land in Okaloosa and Walton Counties, which surround Niceville, is part of the enormous Eglin Air Force Base, which fuels about sixty percent of the local economy. Since the late 1980s the Air Force has been a partner with the cities of Niceville and Valparaiso in promoting the festival as well as facilitating the expansion of the festival site, loaning public address-system equipment and portable bleachers and providing bands and drill teams as part of the entertainment.

(Thundering squadrons of fighter jets on training runs have been a daily occurrence for so long in Niceville that one of the amusing quirks of the natives is that they just start TALKING LOUDER when the planes pass overheard and resume a normal tone of voice when they are gone.)

In recognition of their good civic partner, the 21st Annual Boggy Bayou Mullet Festival in October 1997 was dedicated to the 50th Anniversary of the U.S. Air Force. A commemorative pewter coin was minted, and the graphics for the official logo featured three jets rampant above the festival's name and three mullets rampant below.

For most of its history the festival has been a free event, but a couple of years ago a $1 admission fee was put in place (kids under-12 still free), because, of all reasons (!), a decline in beer sales. But that dollar buys a lot of entertainment. The main stage cranks up at 5 o'clock Friday night and shuts down around midnight; runs from 11 a.m. until midnight on Saturday; starts at 1 p.m. on Sunday, and the last band hits the stage at 5 p.m. Musical offerings include oldies groups, rock, R&B, Cajun, state finalists in the Tru Value/Jimmy Dean Country Showdown, and always a performance by the Niceville High School Golden Eagles Band.

There are eighty-five arts and crafts booths scattered around the site, and over sixty food concessions dish up a staggering variety of good eats: boiled peanuts; funnel cakes; gumbo;

shrimp and other seafood; ostrich burgers; alligator on a stick; international cuisine from Mexico, Greece, Germany, and the Philippines; and of course fried and smoked mullet.

There is everything except a midway. It was the most enjoyable event of its kind that I have ever attended. If the mullet festival in Lillian, Alabama, was like a big family reunion, the Boggy Bayou Mullet Festival is a gigantic community reunion, a celebration of a shared heritage and shared memories that seemed palpable in the dappled sunlight beneath those live oak trees.

●   ●   ●   ●   ●

Though the settlers of Boggy Bayou were from solid Cracker stock, their descendants evolved into a distinct subspecies, preferring to call themselves Boggy Boys. Like the term Fishhead, to be known as a Boggy Boy is a badge of honor, indicative of the pride of place that is so remarkable in this area.

Boggy Boys don't shuffle the dusty streets barefoot and in cutoff dungarees these days (not many of them anyway). And not many of them earn their living by fishing in the bay anymore. They will have a pickup truck (a lot of them equipped with phones) and probably a four-wheel drive sports/utility vehicle to boot and some kind of a boat. They will be avid fishermen and hunters. They will all have a collection of baseball caps, and one of them will be the black one with "Boggy Country, Niceville, Florida" stitched in yellow and four blue-and-silver embroidered mullet jumping out the water. (I have one myself.)

There is, in fact, a kind of country club for Boggy Boys—or an anti-country club, if you will—that celebrates the history and folk culture of Boggy Bayou: The Boggy Boys Sportsman Club (BBSC).

The BBSC has approximately 100 members and maintains a 126-acre reserve right in the heart of the city. They don't do any hunting on their property (oddly, most of the members have hunting camps over in Alabama), but they do keep about 150 foxhounds, deerhounds, and bird dogs penned up there, along with their pet deer. An old yellow yard dog runs loose.

The rustic hunting lodge that serves as their clubhouse was once owned by the Rocky Bayou Sportsman Club and was moved to its present site in 1980. It has a poker room and a cold-drink machine that also dispenses beer. They have a lighted volleyball court. They have a barbecue pit as well as a separate cookhouse, with a smoker for smoking mullet and several large propane-fueled frying tables for frying mullet.

Those frying tables get quite a workout because every year since the Boggy Bayou Mullet Festival began in 1977 the Boggy Boys have manned a fried-mullet concession. They are now synonymous with fried mullet all along the Florida Panhandle, and throughout the year they are in demand to fry a mess of mullet for charity events, political rallies, and private parties. In the process they have become roving ambassadors and public-relations men for the mullet festival.

"We were just a hunting club more than anything else when the festival got started," says James Campbell, one of the two presidents of the sportman's club, the one in charge of the mullet end of things. "About fifteen of us decided we'd cook fish that first year. We came up with about 600 pounds of mullet, and we smoked about 100 pounds of it. We were cooking in little old pots and pans, whatever we could get, and all these people showed up. We sold everything we had.

"Well it took us about a week to get ready for this, a weekend to do it, and then two or three days to get everything closed down. Between drinking the favorite beverages of choice and the hours we put in, it liked to killed every one of us!

"Then the thing started growing. Next thing you know the pots and stoves got bigger—everything is getting bigger, and the poundage is going up. Last year we set a personal record for us. We sold over 10,000 pounds of mullet. There's a lot of people think we are the mullet festival."

● ● ● ● ●

James Campbell, when he can take a break from frying mullet, is director of recreation and emergency management systems for the City of Niceville. He had graciously invited me to hang out with the Boggy Boys as they prepared for the mullet festival, and I had not hesitated in accepting his offer.

The Boggy Boys have stuck with the same menu since Day One: mullet, cheese grits, baked beans, and hush puppies. While their mullet output has greatly increased since 1977, the work crew has been streamlined. Eight Boggy Boys now prepare the food, and their respective wives or girlfriends, wearing Boggy Girl aprons, take the orders and serve up the plates.

Of course there is a steady stream of fellow Boggy Boys who come by to lend a hand or give moral support, which basically means hanging around out back of the food tent, drinking the favorite beverage of choice, and telling old stories, relaying football scores, complaining that there's not enough pepper in the hush puppies, and so forth.

Setting up for the festival starts on Wednesday now, and by Thursday night the cooking-and-serving operation is in place and ready to go. One of the Boggy Girls gave the most appropriate description of this activity when she remarked that "it takes them half an hour and fourteen sayings of 'how's that look?' to get one cooker set up."

●　●　●　●　●

On Thursday night the Chamber of Commerce has a party at the festival site, which includes the annual Mr. Mullet Contest, a parody of a beauty pageant in which contestants camp it up on the festival's main stage in costume and vie for the votes of a panel of judges. I was taking a beer break with one of the Boggy Boys, trying to fill in the rather sketchy description I had been given of the contest, when his young son came bounding up to the table where we were sitting.

"We tried to call you," the boy said, hugging his dad.

"I had my phone turned off. I thought your mother might be trying to call me."

"We did. We tried to call you!"

"That's what I'm trying to tell you, son. That's why I had my phone turned off."

The boy fell silent, obviously wrestling in his mind to decipher what male wisdom might be encoded in the words he'd just heard. "You'll understand before too long," his dad told him.

It was a poignant moment, but I was still a bit in the dark about the Mr. Mullet Contest, and I couldn't curb my tongue.

"What are the benefits of being Mr. Mullet?" I asked.

"Don't know, really. It's either an honor or something you don't want anybody to know about for a year."

●　●　●　●　●

James Campbell has already been Mr. Mullet, and this year all the Boggy Boys are pushing Bruce Price, the director of public works for the City of Niceville, to be selected. There is a "Vote for Bruce" banner on their tent, right by the 9-foot plywood mullet, and they have mounted an intense lobbying campaign on the judges, which amounts to outright bribery actually, showering them with Boggy Boys Sportsman Club shirts and other small gifts, which, evidently, is part of the rules—and the fun.

Bruce seemed to be in fine shape to take the title as he strode onto the stage looking like the archetypal Boggy Boy. He was wearing some camouflage coveralls and rubber hip waders and a Boggy Country baseball cap, and he was carrying a cast net.

The last contestant, an employee at a local bank, came out wearing a suit and tie. He was accompanied by two lovely young ladies, one of whom suddenly went into a swoon and lay down supine on the stage with one arm draped across her face, at which the Mr. Mullet aspirant dashed upstage into a telephone booth that I had not noticed before. He emerged wearing a Superman outfit with a big red "M" instead of an "S" and carrying a good-size mullet, with which he rushed to the fainted damsel and used to resurrect her. (It worked!)

The audience responded with wild applause and whistles and yelps, and I thought it suddenly looked very bad for Bruce's chances. And it was. Super Mullet Man took the title hands down, and Bruce had to settle for First Runner-up.

● ● ● ● ●

I got out to the festival site early Friday morning so I could ride down to Pensacola with James and Bruce to pick up the mullet. As we were about to load up, Don-In-Charge-Of-Cheese-Grits came lumbering up from the main stage area.

"Would you look at this," he said, waving a mullet. "Our new Mr. Mullet left it on the stage. It's been up there all night. Can you believe it? He just left it up there."

"Damn," said Bruce, Mr. First Runner-up. "And you know what? He bought that mullet."

Meaning he didn't catch it himself. Meaning he wasn't really a Boggy Boy at all, just an interloper without the skills to come by a decent mullet without spending money on one. Meaning he didn't deserve to be Mr. Mullet at all. But he was, and Bruce's pals wouldn't let him forget it, ragging him all weekend about being Mr. First Runner-Up.

"I think we ought to return his prop to him," said James, and being the born leader he is, he caught everybody's attention. "I think we ought to return it to him—make a little deposit down at the bank."

Well everybody got to laughing, and it's a good joke and all that, but James wasn't kidding around. He sent one of the crew to get a Ziploc bag, and they found one that's big enough. Bruce and James and I got in the four-wheel drive, and James told me to write a note saying "we're returning the prop you forgot last night" to put in the bag with the mullet, which I did. As we tore off to the bank where Mr. Mullet works, I felt like one of the gang.

When we got to the bank there was another four-wheel in front of us in the drive-up window line, and the woman driving must have been making deposits for half of Niceville—it's like every damn line I ever get in. We sat and sat and sat. While we waited Bruce popped out his cell phone and called his wife,

Boggy Boys Sportsman Club members Jim Paul Davis, James Campbell (a former Mr. Mullet), and Stan Price fried up more than 7,000 pounds of mullet for the 1997 Mullet Festival. Photograph courtesy of Walt Spence, Publicity Director of the Boggy Bayou Mullet Festival.

who happens to be a lawyer, and asked if it's against any state laws to deposit a mullet at a bank drive-up window.

"It don't matter, it don't matter," James said. "We're doing it anyway."

Bruce's wife said no, she didn't think it's against any laws—but for God's sake don't put it in the overnight-deposit box. It would be three days in there by Monday and a stinking mess—if it didn't screw up the machine altogether, which probably is against the law.

"It don't matter," James kept saying. "We're doing it anyway!"

And finally the woman in the four-wheel in line ahead of us

got her receipt for a year's worth of saved pennies, or whatever her business was, and pulled off.

We pulled up to the teller window, and the deposit tray slid out. James put the bag with the mullet in there and said, "We're returning Mr. Mullet's prop." The teller, who had been one of the new Mr. Mullet's onstage assistants the night before, looked at our deposit all big-eyed and said, "Why thank you!" And we tore out laughing our asses off for Pensacola.

An hour later we stopped at a rental lot and picked up a refrigerated truck to store the mullet in over the weekend and then headed to Joe Patty Seafood, where 7,000 pounds of mullet fillets awaited us.

It takes a while to load seventy 100-pound crates of iced-down mullet, so I wandered around the retail market, which has the most extensive selection of seafood I've ever seen outside the Fulton Fish Market in New York City. Several varieties of shrimp, oysters, sushi-grade tuna, grouper, catfish, mahimahi, trigger fish, snapper, amberjack, mackerel, shark, squid, whole mullet and mullet fillets and mullet roe—you name it, and it was on ice. Standing out on the loading dock as Bruce locked down the truck doors, I told the crew chief, "Damn, you got everything that swims in there but octopus."

"We keep that in the freezer," he said.

●　　●　　●　　●　　●

We parked the refrigerated truck full of mullet at the festival site and switched vehicles—one thing these modern Boggy Boys are not short on is vehicles, another is cell phones—and headed to the local Sam's Club to pick up the last of the supplies needed for the weekend: 1,100 pounds of Bush's Best Baked Beans (ninety-eight percent fat free) and 1,300 pounds of something called clear frying oil. I don't know how much cornmeal they used for hush puppies or grits and cheese for the cheese grits because somebody had already bought that stuff.

"I've said this before," James had told me earlier in the week, "I plan on this being my last year of doing this. Not for health reasons, by any means. I'd just like to enjoy the festival one of these days myself."

I could understand what he meant as I watched the operation over that weekend. From morning until late in the evening it was a frenzied pace: Mike mealing down the mullet fillets, Stan and James working the frying tables, Buddy making the hush puppies and Bruce and "Coach" Barfield frying them up, Don stirring up vats of cheese grits, DeWitt keeping the baked beans coming, the Boggy Girls taking orders and serving the dinners and drinks. A night's sleep, and the same thing again. Another night's sleep, and another day like the one before—and then it's all over.

"You won't believe this, Mike," a sweaty and exhausted James Campbell told me late Sunday afternoon, "but we ran out of everything at exactly the same time."

As I was bidding farewell, shaking hands and thanking the guys for sharing this slice of their life with me, James went to his pickup and came back with a parting gift for me. It was one of their club shirts. A beautiful shirt—Hunter green with an embroidered eight-point buck's head surrounded by Boggy Boys Sportsman Club, Nicéville, Florida, stitched in gold.

It was a proud moment for me. I have it dry-cleaned. To avoid shrinkage.

ONLINE MULLETHEADS

I wasn't expecting to find any mullet when I took alternate Highway 19 over to Tarpon Springs. I was on no schedule and wanted a break from the mullet trail really. I definitely wanted a break from the chockablock urban sprawl that begins in earnest around Hudson and Port Richey and runs on south past Tampa Bay.

I had never been to Tarpon Springs, but I knew it was supposed to be a Greek village transposed to the Gulf Coast and was famous for its cantinas and sponges. I remembered Gilbert Roland portraying a Greek sponge diver in a movie called *Underwater* that had been filmed in Tarpon Springs, I think. I saw it, in my preteens, at College Theater on First Avenue 9North in Birmingham—the theater that later became an XXX-rated movie house. I remembered the jaunty angle at which Roland wore his white captain's hat. I remembered his black-and-white striped T-shirt and his white sailor pants. He was always whistling "Cherry Pink and Apple Blossom White," the theme song of the movie. It was a light, airy tune, and I remembered it as if I'd seen the movie yesterday. I started whistling it myself.

The tune was jolted out of my mind, however, when I spied, right on the main drag in Tarpon Springs, a restaurant called The Mullet Boat. A mullethead's work is never done it seems, so I pulled into the parking lot and went inside and struck up a conversation with Costa Tagaropoulis, the owner and chef.

Costa came to Tarpon Springs from Salonika, birthplace of Alexander the Great in northern Greece, when he was fifteen years old. He has owned The Mullet Boat since 1983. Originally the place was just a small shack, out of which was sold takeout mullet that was smoked in the backyard. That space is now the foyer leading to two dining areas with rustic wood paneling and nautical decor that includes beautiful model boats, pulleys and boat propellers, marine-themed paintings, and driftwood. There is a spacious bar where you can watch TV and snack on roasted peanuts. The sound system plays Greek music one minute and Ray Charles the next. The menu lists Greek and American fare, and smoked mullet and mullet spread.

"We kept the name, you know," Costa says, "so we have to have mullet. But it's not always available like it used to be."

In fact it wasn't available during my visit, so I consoled myself with some delicious broiled octopus with sliced fresh tomatoes and a Greek salad, which to my surprise contained potato salad. "Is this a real Greek thing?" I asked Costa.

"No," he said, laughing. "Only in Tarpon Springs. Pappas' [the boss Greek restaurant in town] introduced it a long time ago. Now if it doesn't have potato salad in it, it's not a Greek salad."

I told Costa about my mullet project, and he began laughing again. "There's a group of guys who get together here on Friday nights to drink and have a good time," he told me. "They call themselves the Mullet Heads."

Well my first visit to The Mullet Boat was in August and not on a Friday, and my second visit was in late October and also not on a Friday. I would have liked to attend a meeting of these Mullet Heads, but it did not seem to be in the cards.

During my late-October visit Costa asked, "Do you have E-mail?" He added that the Mullet Heads were into E-mail and he'd pass my address on to them. "Maybe they'll get in touch with you," he said.

I had recently gotten into E-mail mode so I gave Costa my address. Following is the resultant correspondence between myself and former Head Mullet Dale Chappell.

11/8/97

Mike,

Costa from The Mullet Boat restaurant in Tarpon Springs said I should contact you regarding our "Mullet Head" club. Well we were formed about 4 years ago, the result of constantly joking around with Costa about him being the "head" mullet and us (about 14 regulars at the bar on Friday nights) being the "Mullet Heads." One thing led to another, and all of a sudden the Mullet Heads club was born.

Basically we are a social club which has absolutely no purpose for existence or rules to abide by. Our mission is to get together and have a good time. Every year at Christmas time during our annual party we elect a new "Head Mullet." It's the Head Mullet's job to protect the tradition of the Mullet Heads and to be the keeper of the sacred gifts from previous Head Mullets. So far we have assembled the following items:

1994—Head Mullet Jim Rains (he's actually the inventor of the Mullet Heads but he denies it) invented the "holy lighted antlers."

1995—Head Mullet Dale Chappell (me) invented the "lighted candle hat" and "sacred lighted cape."

1996—Head Mullet Mickey Flowers. So far he hasn't told us what he is inventing, but he sort of wrecked the lighted antlers and lighted hat. He has promised to "refurbish" these items and get them in working order for the party. We'll be lucky if he remembers to bring the stuff to the party.

It's reported this year that Jim and Dale are working on a secret project that may involve a snowman with a lighted mullet fish-head hat.

We also have the holy Christmas tree. It's only 8 inches high, but it is lighted by 2 strings of battery-operated lights. Every Mullet Head pays homage to the tree, and they all place gifts around it. Everyone goes "oooh" and "ahhh" when they see the tree.

We are constantly searching for new members. Most of us are close to 50. Some are over 50. A couple are approaching 70 . . . the youngest just turned 40. We are a diverse group, coming from upstate New York, Baltimore, Atlanta, St. Louis, Boston, and parts unknown.

Our Christmas party this year is on Friday, Dec. 19, at The Mullet Boat. I've heard a rumor that there may be a mullet-tossing contest on that date too. That's about all I can think of to say right now.

Dale

11/11/97

Dale,

thanks for making contact. the info on you guys is more than welcome. if i wasn't such a mullethead, i would have made a meeting. i was in the area, and it slipped my mind about the friday night meetings until i showed up at costa's on the saturday after.

work on the book has me really swamped, and today is a bad day for all i'd like to talk to you about. i think a chapter about your branch of mulletheads via e-mail would be a good thing as my deadline looms and it is doubtful i can make another trip as far south as tarpon springs. give me a couple days to straighten out some things on my end, and i'll be back in contact.

in case you didn't see the article i did for the Village Voice, i'll forward it from another file.

again, great to hear from you. all the best.

michael swindle

12/15/97

Dale,

hope this finds you doing well. it looks like i might be coming down to the homosassa area to go out on a mullet roe run in a couple of days. which would put me close to tarpon springs on the 19th for the mullet heads' annual party.

is it still on the 19th? will it be held at costa's? would it be alright for me to attend if things work out on my end?

let me know. look forward to hearing from you.

michael

12/15/97

Michael,

Yes, we are having the xmas party at Costa's. Everyone is all excited about it, and everyone is making their hat, costume, etc. for the party. Everyone is trying to find out what the other person is making this year.

I cut out the shape of a mullet from Styrofoam and glued it to the top of an old pink Easter hat my wife had and decorated it with battery-operated blinking lights, topped off with a mini xmas tree and 6 small Santas marching toward the front of the mullet. It also has plastic icicles hanging from the back, along with a red bow glued to the mullet's tail. IT'S UNBELIEVABLE. I call it "THE CHRISTMAS MULLET."

I also took a piece of pipe, covered it with tinfoil, and decorated it with battery-operated lights. I call it "THE GUIDED LIGHT."

I know that Jim and Ann have cooked up something special, and so have Mickey and Dottie (he's the Head Mullet this year).

Costa is having a DJ play some music, and Pappa John is making kielbasa and kraut plus some other munchies. So far we have almost 20 people coming . . . about 12 Mullet Heads and some friends. It would be great if you could stop by . . . bring your camera. It's going to be a sight to behold. THIS WILL BE THE BIG EVENT IN TARPON SPRINGS!!!!!!!! It sounds like it will be our best party yet.

Dale

I/II/98

Dale,

as i'm sure you noticed, i did not make it down your way for the annual christmas party. it really killed me, but it was just not meant to be.

i'm sure you guys had a grand time. i'm frantically trying to finish the book, having missed the original deadline (only about 65% finished). the whole shebang must be ready to go to press by the end of this month.

what i'd like to do is have a chapter called "cyber mulletheads" or something like that, that would consist of our e-mail correspondence. your messages are very descriptive and the whole thing is such great fun!

what do you think of the idea? I have a few questions: could you give me a little more description of your "lighted candle hat" and the "sacred lighted cape"? what do you do in "real life"? same for jim rains and mickey flowers? did mickey flowers "refurbish" the sacred mullet items? what did he come up with this year? did you have a mullet toss? also i'm eager to hear your version of how the party went.

if all this is not a pain for you, i look forward to your next e-mail. then i'll give you a telephone call and we can do a short interview or whatever. maybe i should talk to a couple of the other head mullets or the newest one. we'll see.

happy new year, and i'll talk to you soon.

michael

p.s. i tried to e-mail costa, but the message was returned. i guess

Costa Tagaropoulis, owner and chef of The Mullet Boat in Tarpon Springs, wearing the Christmas Mullet hat and holding the "holy guided light scepter" at the Mullet Heads 1997 Christmas party. Photograph courtesy of Dale Chappell, former Head Mullet.

i'll try him again and see if i can get through. in any case, please give him my regards. does he still do his newsletter? later.

1/12/98

Michael,

This year's party was terrific. You had to be there to appreciate what happened. Everybody had the "hat fever."

As soon as I can find a scanner, I'll send you the pictures. I also have forwarded your mail to some of the "online" Mullet Heads. Hopefully they'll be contacting you soon.

Mickey revamped the "lighted candle" hat . . . he did a great job and added a lot of personal touches. I created the "Christmas Mullet" hat this year. I carved a mullet out of Styrofoam, glued it to an old Easter bonnet, put battery-operated lights on each side, glued six miniature santa clauses to the top, glued a tiny xmas tree to the top, and had a cigar hanging out of the mouth. IT WAS A HOOT.

I also created the "holy guided light scepter" this year. It was a piece of pipe covered with tinfoil and covered with battery-operated lights. It's in a few pictures. The new Head Mullet, Larry Lang, was crowned with it during the ceremony.

Jim Rains came up with a hat that had a shark attached to the top and also was covered with lights. His wife, Ann, had the same thing. Jim got dressed up in red shorts, red suspenders, and a red plaid shirt.

Mickey and Dottie came all dolled up in red outfits, complete with tinsel hanging all over them. Mickey also had a pair of red xmas balls hanging in a strategic place just below his belt buckle. He definitely redeemed himself for destroying the lighted candle hat.

Even the barmaid (Georgia) got into it this year . . . she had a pair of antlers on her head and was dressed in xmas attire. Everyone is already talking about what they are going to do for the next party . . . IT'S GREAT . . . everybody's got the fever this early in the year already . . . There's rumors that the hats will talk next xmas.

As for me, I am a computer programmer . . . I took early retirement from IBM after 24 years in NY back in 1992 and now work as a supervisor in a system support group for our mainframe systems at Nielsen Media Research (the TV ratings people) here in Florida. As far as my e-mail address goes, I was a volunteer firefighter for 19 years back home in NY (Hudson Valley - Orange County). I ended up being one of the fire chiefs of the company and was one year away from being THE fire chief before IBM decided to move me upstate to Endicott in 1992. When IBM moved me I decided that it was time to get out and go south . . . So we did . . . and here we are!

No mullet toss this year, but something may happen in 1998. I'll check with Costa about his e-mail . . . He was having trouble with it . . . Take care . . . talk to you soon.

Dale

THE MELVILLE OF MULLET

I guess you could say that the Red Roe Restaurant, located on Banana Creek in the small "former fishing village" of Ozona, found me instead of the other way around. It called to me—and thank God I heard it.

Driving south out of Tarpon Springs toward Clearwater one bright and beautiful fall afternoon, I saw an advertisement for the place painted in red on a white bench at a bus stop on the side of the highway. The name jumped out at me. It had the ring of mullet about it. And well it should have I learned in talking to the owner, Leslie Alfred.

Although the Red Roe has such items on the menu as gumbo, New Zealand green mussels, alligator bites, Alaskan snow crab, and stuffed flounder, the specialty of the house is smoked mullet. The restaurant is on the site of what was once Hart's Fish Market, where mullet fishermen used to bring their catch up Banana Creek. It's a bird sanctuary now, but back in those days it was an open estuary to the bay. Mullet skiffs were once built in the space that is now the dining room.

"My former husband and I opened this place ten years ago," Leslie told me. "He's also a writer, and the restaurant was named for one of his novels, *Red Roe Run*, about mullet fishing on the west coast of Florida right after World War II. He just published a book called *Man & Mullet*."

Well the little "ring of mullet" I'd heard out on the highway turned into a fire alarm going off in my head. I started machine-gunning questions: He did what? When did it come out? What's his name? Who published the book? Where can I get one? How can I get in touch with him?

"Like I said," she told me, a bit icily, "he's my former husband. I don't talk to him that often. His name is Alan Frederiksen, and he lives up in Homosassa."

And that was pretty much the end of that conversation.

● ● ● ● ●

I held my breath as I waited for the information operator to tell me whether or not there was a listing for Alan Frederiksen in Homosassa, and I was a happy guy as I wrote down the number the computer-generated voice croaked out to me. I reached him on the first try and made an appointment to see him on my trip home from Sarasota.

Alan had suggested I stay at a place called McRae's, right on the river in "historic downtown Homosassa," but I arrived after nine in the evening only to find that the main office closes down at seven. Luckily there was a Howard Johnson motor lodge just downriver. The ambience was far less rustic than McRae's, but they did have a vacancy—and I took it.

As I was settling into my room I heard music coming from somewhere, lively music with the lilting tones of a steel drum. I walked outside to investigate, and I could see on the opposite bank of the river a well-lighted cabana-bar where a band was playing to a festive crowd. It was an inviting scene and seemed a perfect way to end the night. However, as I paced the bank on my side of the river, I could discern no way to get across.

I saw a young couple sitting on a bench by the tennis court and asked, "How does one get across the river from here?"

"Well sir," the young fellow answered, "you can drive down about nine miles to the bridge and cross over or you can swim."

● ● ● ● ●

Homosassa is about as Old Florida as any place you'll find, located in what is called "the rain forest of West Florida." The name "Homosassa," according to Allen Morris in his book *Florida Place Names,* refers to a group of islands, a bay, a point, a river, and a spring that has a flow of 70,000 gallons per minute. Seminoles lived in the area in the early 1800s, and one view is that the name comes from two Indian words that mean "a place where peppers grow." Another etymological faction, however, holds that the name means "smoking creek" because of the fog that forms on the warm springs and the river whenever the temperature drops.

Alan Frederiksen lives right in the middle of this rain forest, in three small fishing cabins on a 2-acre compound carved out of the lush vegetation between Mason Creek and the Homosassa River, where he traps blue crabs, fishes for mullet, chops swamp cabbage (the heart of a local palm tree) for dinner, and writes.

Frederiksen was born in Copenhagen. He came to this country in 1936 when he was two years old. His father, who traveled the world as a ship's officer in the maritime service, had fallen in love with Indian Rocks Beach near Clearwater because the dunes reminded him of the dunes on the North Sea. He decided to settle there with his wife and child. "It was a wild and wonderful place back in those days," Alan says. "The dunes are long gone, of course. It's nothing but a concrete canyon now."

After serving in World War II, the elder Frederiksen opened a fish house at Indian Rocks Beach, so Alan from a young age has had an intimate knowledge of commercial fishing. His father fished for grouper not mullet, and Alan assisted him in that activity on occasion. But it was not until he was thirty-six years old that he became a fisherman himself.

In the interim he attended the University of Florida where he studied with the noted writer and critic Andrew Lytle, whom he acknowledges as his mentor, and decided to become a writer himself. For ten years he lived in the French Quarter in New Orleans where he wrote and published the novel *Love & Guilt*, which is now out of print.

By the end of the 1970s he had a young son and daughter and decided the beaches of West Florida would be a better place to raise them than the French Quarter. He moved back to his old stomping ground at Indian Rocks Beach and opened a fish house, out of which he crabbed and gill-netted mullet. In the late 1980s he and his wife, Leslie, opened the Red Roe Restaurant.

Red Roe Run, published in 1983, is also out of print, although as Alan likes to say "it is available in libraries throughout the nation." It is a complex book. On one level it is an authentic and minutely detailed description of what mullet fishing was like on Florida's West Coast during the time between World War II and the Korean War.

On another level it is the coming-of-age story of one Garwood Winetrout, his star-crossed love of a local girl, and his confrontation with "a terrible fact" buried in his family's history. There is humor and tragedy in equal measure. There is even supernatural sex involving a professional snake milker.

Above all there is the brooding evocation of "a homogeneous clan-society beginning its death-throe," of an old way of life being inexorably ground down by the milling stones of development and population explosion.

Two sections of the novel appeared in the summer and winter issues of the respected journal *The Sewanee Review* in 1970. Despite that auspicious beginning, when Alan finished the novel he could not find a publisher willing to take a chance on the book, so he had it published independently.

"Mainstream publishing is in a sad state these days," he says. "I chalk it up to the vagaries of the short attention span. But on the other hand, as Truman Capote used to say, a boy has to hustle his book."

In 1991 Alan and Leslie divorced, and he sold out his interest in the restaurant. He moved to his fish camp in Homosassa and did nothing but write for three years, finishing two novels that ultimately displeased him and that he put aside before going back to crabbing and gill-netting mullet to earn a living.

"Writing is a great way to starve," he says, with a loud and hearty laugh. "Hell, I've made more money in one week of netting mullet during the roe season than I've made in my whole life writing!"

Another book that he finished in those years of writing, however, was a keeper: *Man & Mullet*, published, again independently, in 1995. Subtitled *An Elegy for a Lost Way of Life* the book is a masterful piece of work. It is his *Moby Dick* and establishes him as the Melville of the mullet world.

It is, to quote from the flyleaf, "a word and pictorial narrative of the infringement increased human population has had upon a way of life traditional and honorable: gill-netting mullet on Florida's West Coast. A true story tracing adversary user groups: waterfront homeowners and recreational fishermen allied against the commercial fishing community. This Florida battle pitting user groups for a declining natural resource is symbolic of the worldwide pressure upon our environmentally stressed planet. There are no victors in this contest: Life and the living are the losers."

This may sound polemical—and the book is certainly that, but it is considerably more. There is nothing about mullet and fishing for mullet that cannot be found in this book. It is also highly personal, built around entries from actual logs Frederiksen kept of his fishing trips over several years, amongst which are interspersed passages of history and remembrance that he has given what he calls "a fictive tension."

"You have to watch that narrator," he warns. "Everything in the logs is true, but that narrator who comes in, everything he says may not be the 'truth.' It's imagination at work. And imagination is the only real truth. That's personally the way I view it."

The unique diction of Frederiksen's characters is another thing that stands out in his work. I have never heard people speak the way he has them speaking. It can be awkward when you begin reading him, but once you catch the rhythm it becomes just another pleasure.

"Some people have said it sounds Elizabethan," he told me when I asked about it. "But I don't know about that. I think one reason may be found in those years long ago when I had to translate English into Danish for my mother. Again I don't know. The bottom line is that I'm not sure the fishermen I've written about talked the way I have them talk, but by God that's the way they ought to talk!"

TED PETERS
FAMOUS SMOKED FISH

I was talking with Grif Griffin, a fellow writer who lives in Old Town, and his admonition was brief and direct: "You gotta go to Ted Peters Famous Smoked Fish down in St. Petersburg. They have the best smoked mullet in the world."

Now first of all, when Grif tells you anything about Florida, you better take heed because his opinions come from years of roaming over every part of the state.

Second, the old saying about sex also applies to smoked mullet: The worst you ever get is going to be pretty good. So if somebody is talking about The Best and it's being offered . . . well who could resist?

I called ahead to see if I could get an audience with Ted Peters himself and thought I had been granted one until I arrived at the restaurant in Pasadena Beach and found myself talking to one Michael Lathrop.

"This is a fine way to begin a relationship," I told him, "with a lie."

"I didn't lie," he replied with an impish grin. "You asked for Ted. I came on the phone. During our conversation you asked me if I was the owner, and I said yes. And I am one of the owners."

It was precisely the kind of insouciant parsing one would expect from a bred-in-the-bone mullethead, which he readily admitted that he was, and from that moment on the two of us got along . . . well, famously.

Ted Peters Famous Smoked Fish—also known as Mullethead Heaven—
serves the definitive smoked mullet and the definitive smoked mullet spread.

Lathrop's father, it turned out, was Ted Peters's half brother and his original partner in the restaurant that has been operating in its present location since 1951. The place is definitely of its time, what used to be called a drive-in: a one-story concrete building surrounded by a shell parking lot, with open-air dining at picnic tables along the front and the south side. (The original smoker is in a detached building across the parking lot.) Other than new coats of paint and a minor tweak here and there, it is unchanged from the time it was built.

"Back in the 1970s we talked about remodeling," Lathrop told me, "but we decided it was a bad idea. We are going into the twenty-first century kicking and screaming. We know how to use the wheel. We know how to use fire. We don't need much else."

● ● ● ● ●

Ted Peters is eighty-six-years old now, and while he retains his interest in the restaurant he is not involved in the day-to-day operations. He is too busy having fun. The guy maintains the social schedule of someone half his age. He stayed one jump ahead of me during my first trip to St. Petersburg, and I practically had to stake out his house to catch him when I returned a couple of months later.

("My dad was the serious one," says Michael Lathrop. "Even if we were just going out in the boat, there had to be a purpose—getting somewhere, fishing, whatever. It was ninety percent business and ten percent fooling around. When you went out in a boat with Ted, it was all fooling around.")

Ted was not the first one to smoke mullet in southwestern Florida of course. That had been going on at least since the time of the Calusa Indians, a highly sophisticated and civilized tribe that dominated the area centuries before any Europeans arrived on the scene. The Calusa actually built stone holding pens in which they "farmed" mullet. They also had large sailing craft they used for trading as far south as Cuba and the Bahamas. And it was from a wound inflicted by a Calusa poisoned arrow that Juan Ponce de Leon died in 1521.

(They were also manatee eaters, according to Michael Lathrop. "They called it sea pork and said it really tasted good. Though you probably wouldn't want to put that in your book." No, I told him, I "probably wouldn't." He's not the only insouciant parser around, and now we're even.)

"I didn't know anything about mullet before we came down here from upstate New York right after World War II," Ted says.

"But I learned a lot about it. My stepbrother had captain's papers out of Madeira Beach, running a boat out of there, so I got into the fish business with him. And there was an old smoker outside the fisherman's cooperative—we started out with that.

"I was a marketer, more or less, when we started. I had no education, but I had a little aggressiveness. What little fish they smoked around here, they did it out in the woods or out in the backyard, where people never saw it. Well I said, 'Put it out there where people can see that thing.'"

Next Ted acquired what he still calls a "gin mill," The Blue Anchor, out on Blind Pass. He put a smoker right out on the highway. Cars passing by would have to slow down as they approached the bridge, and when they did Ted would haul out a tray of smoked mullet and most of the time make a sale.

"At the original smokehouse," he says, chuckling at the memory, "they had a pay telephone inside, and outside there was a sign that showed an emblem of a telephone booth. People were always stopping and saying, 'Hey, your telephone booth is on fire!'"

Peters moved on from The Blue Anchor and ran a joint called Bayside Tavern for a while before he and Michael's father opened Ted Peters Famous Smoked Fish in Pasadena Beach near St. Petersburg in 1951.

The men filled in the land on the lot where the restaurant still sits, hauling rocks and sand and building walls so that what they had built up would stay put because it "was just something you did, and you went and did it."

The times were pretty wild in those days in South Florida. The state legislature passed a law that regulated bar hours in unincorporated areas like South Pasadena. Incorporated towns, on the other hand, could set their own bar-closing laws, which effectively meant bars didn't have to close at all. Pasadena decided to incorporate, but during the legal process, much to the dismay of bar owners and customers alike, it was discovered that the town didn't qualify for incorporation. There weren't twenty-nine permanent residents!

"So that was the end of that," says Ted. "It was pretty hilarious."

Over the years there have been numerous offers to franchise the operation, but they were all turned down. It supported the family just the way it was, with Michael's father and Ted alternately working a month on and a month off, which is just the kind of workload any self-respecting mullethead would relish.

Ted puts it simply: "It worked out."

● ● ● ● ●

There are people who ate their first smoked mullet at Ted Peters and now bring their grandchildren. And if there's any justice in this world, those grandchildren will be bringing their children's children in the future.

The reason is simple: Ted Peters Famous Smoked Fish is Mullethead Heaven. I ate a considerable amount of smoked mullet in 1997, and the product at Ted Peters was hands down, no contest, the absolute best. The fish are big and meaty, redolent of wood smoke yet succulent.

The Famous Smoked Mullet dinner comes with German potato salad, rye bread and butter, pickles, tomato, sweet onion, lemon, and coleslaw. You can buy smoked mullet to go priced by the pound, and I wouldn't pass up the smoked mullet spread, available by the half pint, pint, and quart. (They also serve a killer Manhattan-style clam chowder jazzed up Southern style. Have a cup as an appetizer.)

Neither Michael Lathrop nor Ted Peters is very forthcoming about the "trade secrets" that separate their mullet from the rest of the herd. The mullet's environment is very important, they say, and the best mullet come from the local waters where there is a nice sandy bottom. (Ironically, people all along the coast—Niceville, Apalachicola, Cedar Key, Homosassa—told me the exact same thing. As if there were only one stretch of sandy bottom in the whole state.)

You want a mullet with a heavy layer of body fat, they say. Proper processing is key, and they have very exacting standards.

"For years we only used buttonwood for smoking the fish," Ted Peters told me. "It is one of the three growth phases of mangrove. Right down at the waterline you have red mangrove, and just in back of that is the black mangrove. Neither has qualities for smoking. Behind the black mangrove, up on the higher ground, was the buttonwood. That was excellent, sweet smoke. That's all we used. If you cut that now you'd get thrown in jail and you'd never get out!"

Now they use red oak and "hot smoke" the mullet, meaning the fish is smoked in wire-mesh trays directly over the fire. (Hot smoking, by the way, is the method that is virtually universal for smoking mullet.)

So there you have it. That's how you make the best smoked mullet in the world.

BLUE IN CORTEZ

When I told Michael Lathrop, of Ted Peters Famous Smoked Fish, that I was going to take a ride down to Cortez, he paused for a moment and told me, "You are going to the vortex of mullet." As I have found to be true throughout my brief association with him, Lathrop knew what he was talking about.

The small fishing village of Cortez is located at the tip of a broad peninsula just north of Sarasota and west of Bradenton. In its earliest days the area was known as Hunter's Point, but when a post office was officially opened in 1888 the town was named after the Spanish explorer, which is curious because the area was settled by commercial fishermen of English descent, the majority of whom migrated from the coastal counties of North Carolina. (Come to think of it, why wasn't the area originally known as "Fishers' Point"?)

The early Cortezians referred to the eastern shore of Sarasota Bay, to the south of them, as "The Kitchen" because of the huge quantities of fish, scallops, and other seafood they harvested there. The core of the fishing industry, however, was unquestionably netting the enormous schools of black mullet. Thousands upon thousands of pounds of mullet were caught out of Cortez. Early on the fish were processed and shipped north to Cedar Key, which was a terminus for the first trans-Florida railroad. When the railroad finally arrived in Tampa, most of the fish were rerouted to that much closer city.

Cortez was virtually destroyed by a hurricane in 1921, but the fish houses and other shoreline structures were rebuilt. Even today there is a feeling of another time to this quiet little fishing town.

A big part of the quiet unfortunately is due to the banning of the traditional gill nets back in 1995. The ban is still very much a sore spot in the fishing community, and because of the restrictive new laws the harvest of mullet out of Cortez is a mere shadow of what it was in the old days.

The full impact of the situation hit me on the October afternoon I paid a visit to the A. P. Bell Fish Company, the oldest and largest wholesale fish house in the area. The workers were processing mullet that had come from North Carolina. This fact added poignancy to the weathered sign I had seen down the street from Bell's proclaiming the town's credo: "Cast your nets and feed the multitudes."

One of the reasons I had come to Cortez was to see Karen Bell, a vivacious, intelligent young woman whose family opened the A. P. Bell Fish Company in 1940. She works in the business but has recently branched out. She bought the Star Fish Company, a retail seafood operation next door to Bell's, to which I had been told she had added a restaurant, with smoked mullet a prime offering.

Foolishly I had not called ahead, and Karen had to inform me that her restaurant would not be open for another month and that she could not spare me the time I would have liked on this particular day to talk about mullet.

She turned out to be vitally helpful, however, when I told her that another reason for my visit was to see Blue Fulford, an older mullet fisherman who lived in town.

"Oh really," she said. "You didn't tell me you knew Blue. He's definitely the man you should be talking to."

"Well," I told her, "I don't really know him. He was recommended by a couple of people I met recently."

"Do you know where his house is?" she asked.

When I answered again in the negative, she picked up the phone and dialed Blue's number from memory. She passed a few pleasantries with him and then told him she had a writer in her office who would like to come over to see him if he had the time.

"Says he's out on his dock, messing with some nets," Karen said, hanging up the phone. "Says come on over."

She quickly drew me a simple map to his house, and I thanked her for her assistance. The mullet world these days can be highly charged, and cold calls to fishermen or fish house owners always have the capability of turning sour on you. Karen's phone introduction made me feel a lot better about this visit.

Blue Fulford lives on a quiet cul-de-sac off the main road through Cortez, just before you get to the bridge that takes you to Bradenton Beach and Longboat Key, in a well-kept one-story brick house that was built by mullet. The yard is immaculately trimmed and runs to a canal behind the house. Blue has a boathouse out there, with a workshop and a covered patio area where he can sit and relax and listen to big mullet plopping in the water.

Blue is a medium-size, compact man in his early seventies who walks with a slight limp. His voice tends toward the high register, with a lilting twang to it that I would call a "hill country" accent if he were from Mississippi. He speaks slowly and chooses his words carefully, and he has a dry sense of humor that often bubbles to the surface in his conversation. The word "dignified" comes to mind.

"Name is Fulford," he says in greeting, "one L. First name's Blue."

"Somebody told me it was Thomas," I tell him.

"Well my momma called me Sonny," he counters chuckling. "People used to say, 'Sonny's name is Tommy, but they call him Blue.'"

When I met Blue I knew that he had fished mullet for several decades and that he had been a vocal and effective spokesman against the gill net ban, though his efforts ultimately failed. I did not know, nor did he bring it up, that he had actually been the executive director of OFF, Organized Fishermen of Florida, one of two trade organizations that lobby the Florida state legislature on issues concerning the commercial-fishing industry. As it turned out it was not the only thing I wouldn't learn about the man until later.

We sat down at a table on the dockside patio, and Blue began to tell me about his fishing days but quickly sidetracked to the topic that is inescapable in the mullet world: the net ban. "I had an open cockpit boat I used, with an inboard motor," he told me. "Always liked to fish that kind of boat. Never did like a kicker boat—a boat with an outboard motor mounted in the bow so you can work a net out of the stern. 'Round here we called 'em 'bird dogs.'

"That's one reason we got the net ban. They made it where too many people could fish, and they had no concern for the people, the sportsmen, who were out there. They'd just get out and run around anywhere they wanted to. Didn't have to have any experience—they'd come and go fishing one time with somebody with a kicker boat, and then the fish dealer would buy this greenhorn one if he wanted one. Seemed like that's the way it was.

"Had these monofilament nets. Didn't have to mend them like the old cotton nets, didn't have to dry them and bleach them at the end of every day. Just pull it on the boat and pull it off when you got through with it at the end of the year. Just made it available to too many people, made it more mobile.

"If there was an area had a few fish in it and somebody heard about it, here come fifteen or twenty new kicker boats from another area in there, back down to the loading ramp, load up, and take off somewhere.

"I never did go down, but they told me down around Everglades and Naples in roe run season two or three years before the net ban, there'd be as many as 400 boats down there congregated on that area, fishing everywhere they could. It just put too much pressure on the fisheries."

Back when he was fishing Blue used a 24-foot open-cockpit launch during the roe season. He liked that kind of boat because, during that time of year when they are spawning, mullet are schooled up in huge "knots." They are moving around, and they're in deep water.

"In the summertime I had that skiff sitting right there," he said, pointing to the small craft in the nearby boat shed. "I'd put my net on that skiff, and I'd tow it to where I wanted to fish. Then I'd anchor the launch and get in the skiff with a 14-foot poling oar. I'd pole to where I wanted to go and strike the net.

"I had a couple thousand yards of net that I'd run by myself. Most of the time there'd be four men on that much net. You had to fish up against a shore somewhere; it's hard to make a round strike, just one man, and catch fish. You'd have to get up against a shore or in a canal where you could cut them off.

"There were plenty of areas like that to fish around here, all these canals and seawalls. I seen some places it would be hard to make a living pole-skiffing just one man. But around here it worked out pretty good. I liked that way of fishing. Off to yourself. Nobody in your way. You make a mistake, you didn't have anybody to blame it on. Talked to myself a lot."

Before the Skyway Bridge provided a land route to Tampa and St. Pete, Blue would sometimes join two or three other fishermen and do what they called "ice fishing." The crew used a large launch, one with a fish box aboard large enough to hold 4,000 pounds of fish. They would load up with enough ice to keep their catch fresh over several days and head by water up to Tampa Bay. They towed several poling skiffs from which they would net mullet and then transfer them into the iced fish boxes on the larger vessel. That kind of fishing passed away with the coming of the bridge because people could simply hook boats to their trucks and drive over to that stretch of water.

"Lots of things are changing," Blue says quietly.

Things are changing indeed. Blue has two sons who fish with gill nets—but not for mullet. They fish for bait: red herring and sardines. Three miles offshore; the only place it's legal.

But one thing that isn't going to change in Florida any time soon, if ever, is the net ban. Unlike the other Gulf Coast states that passed laws banning or restricting the use of gill nets,

Florida's ban was accomplished by passing an amendment to the state constitution.

And that was always the plan of the antinetters, led by large, wealthy, powerful sportfishermen's associations, according to Blue, who speaks for commercial fishermen in this issue more eloquently and rationally than anyone else I met in my travels.

"They wanted the ban chiseled in stone," he tells me, "where you couldn't move it, where you couldn't do anything with it. That was one of the evils of it. You could stand regulation. You could even stand a moratorium if you had to, to let fish stocks rebuild. But something like this? Where you've got to get 450,000 people to sign a petition that they want to change the state constitution and then get out and have an election and get people voting who don't know a blamed thing in the world about fishing?

"That's what used to scare me to death. I'd ride up and down these highways, and everywhere I'd look you'd see a new apartment complex going up. I mean, all those people don't know a thing about fishing. They haven't been in Florida but just long enough to move in. And they are going to be asked what to do on my livelihood? That's just not right! It might have been legal, but it wasn't right."

Blue went silent, and as he did a loud splash from a jumping mullet sounded just off the dock, catching our attention. We both turned and watched the widening ripples of its wake until the water was still again.

"They don't come up in here like they did when the nets were fishing," Blue said. "When the nets were out there all the time, mullet would run up in places like this, but now there's nothing out there to aggravate them. They stay out there and play."

Blue went silent again before picking up his thought. "They're just behaving a whole different way from what they used to. But it wouldn't take them long to get back up here if they opened it up for netting again."

And then he paused again. "But I don't ever want them to open it up like it was though," he said, thinking, I guessed, of those kicker boats he didn't like and the greenhorns driving them. "I wouldn't care if they did away with gill nets myself. We could catch them with seines."

And then another pause before he gently clapped his hands on his knees and rose from his chair, signaling he'd had enough of talking for one afternoon. "Ah well," he said, "I don't really think much about fishing these days."

He said it, but who could believe him?

● ● ● ● ●

Leaving Cortez I stopped at the Sea Horse Oyster Bar and Grill on the eastern edge of town. A large yellow banner with bold black letters proclaiming "Draft Beer, 75 cents" had caught my eye. A cold beer sounded mighty fine, and the price fit my budget.

There were only two customers at the far end of the bar, and that suited me. I wasn't much in the mood for conversation after my visit with Blue Fulford, so I settled on the first high-back stool and placed my order.

I was pretty much lost in my own thoughts, but I couldn't help hearing some of the conversation of the two young guys down the bar. The word "mullet" jerked me back into the present.

"Excuse me," I said. "Did I hear you say you fished for mullet?"

The fellow closest to me turned in my direction. He was a burly piece of business, wearing a black, flat-top Clint Eastwood Stetson, work clothes, and white rubber boots, the kind that all the shrimpers in South Louisiana wear.

"Yeah."

"I'm writing a book about mullet."

"Is that right," he said. "Well are you with 'em or against 'em?"

The question confused me for a moment, and I foolishly asked who he meant.

"The commercial fishermen," he sneered.

"I, I'm with them," I declared, but my half stammer only riled him more.

"Yeah, right," he spat back. "Well let me tell you something. They're trying to run us out of here. The Yankee land developers and the sportfishers and their damned scientists. I've lived here all my life and I've fished all my life and I ain't going nowhere! These scientists trying to tell us what's happened to all the fish, trying to put it on us! You think people that's lived here all their lives don't know what's happened to all the fish? It's the runoff from all the hotels and condos and golf courses. I know where you can put your scientists and his test tubes! Put that in your goddam book!"

With that he pushed out of his stool. Coming for me I thought, but he stormed past me and out the door. Leaving behind a heavy silence.

Photograph by Underwood & Underwood/Corbis-Bettmann.

I quickly finished my beer and threw four bucks on the bar.

Walking to the car I thought, a little too late, about a sign I had seen in cafes and bars all up and down the Gulf Coast. It said: Not even a fish would get in trouble if it kept its mouth shut!

● ● ● ● ●

It had been on the advice of Alan "the Melville of Mullet" Frederiksen that I had gone to Cortez to see Blue Fulford. The next time I saw Alan I related my encounter at the Sea Horse. "I looked at my dance card," I told him, "and wallowing on a barroom floor with a big ol' mullethead wasn't on there."

"Well hell, anybody from north of Gainesville is a Yankee!" he said after he finished laughing. "Did you ask Blue about how he lost his leg?" he wanted to know.

"I noticed he had a limp," I said. "He even said his leg was hurting. But for some reason I never got around to asking him about it. What happened?"

"He was out with a crew purse seining for bait fish," Alan told me. "Blue got his leg caught in what they call the donkey collar, a steel piece that tightens down on the seine to compress the fish in the net. He would have been hauled into the gears and killed—it was just about all over. But he's a hell of a man. He yelled, 'Take the leg!' And it was his son cut Blue's foot off. Saved his life."

It was a while before I could speak, and then all I could think to say was, "So much for my investigative reporter skills. What a mullethead!"

"Aw hell, Michael," Alan said. "You'd only just met the man."

A "mullet wrapper" circling his net. Photograph by Winston Luzier.

MULLET CHOKING

Winston Luzier is a professional photographer who shoots everything from rocket launches at Cape Canaveral to Tampa Bay Buccaneer games for Reuters News Service, as well as doing freelance work for various fishing and boating magazines. He is also the old University of Florida roommate who pinned the nickname "Mullet" on Dave Martin, the AP photographer who ran afoul of the law in Montgomery, Alabama, for throwing dead fish.

"You want to talk to a serious mullethead," Dave had told me, "call Winston down in Sarasota."

So I did call Winston, and Dave was right.

"When I first met Dave," Winston told me, "he announced that he was a slob, and he wasn't lying, man. It only took a couple of days of being his roommate until it hit me. I told him he was just an old mullet, and the nickname stuck. My dad had called me 'Mullet Choker' since I was a little kid, so Dave and I made quite a pair. The Mullet and the Mullet Choker."

"How did you come by such a gruesome-sounding sobriquet?" I asked him.

"Why don't you come down for a couple of days," he replied, "and I'll give you a demonstration instead of a description."

● ● ● ● ●

The original plan had been for us to walk a couple blocks from Winston's house over to Sarasota Bay and have him wade in with his cast net and get a mess of mullet, but that was too simple for a mullethead of his caliber. He had arranged for us to meet an old friend and commercial fisherman, Boaty Boatwright, and go out in his boat instead.

"That old saying is true," Winston said, as we drove south out of Sarasota. "There's nothing like messing about in boats. Besides Boaty is just the best at throwing a cast net."

Winston was in high spirits, and as we wove through traffic, he told me about his dream of opening a mullet joint. "I'm gonna call it the Flip-Flop Inn," he said. "Serve nothing but smoked mullet and smoked mullet backbones and beer. The hook is that you have to have on a pair of flip-flops to get in, and if you don't have any, we'll sell you a pair."

●　　●　　●　　●　　●

We put Boaty's small Carolina skiff in the water at Blackburn Point near the old turnkey bridge over to Casey Key. Boaty grew up on these waters and knows them as well as anyone possibly could. As a kid in the 1940s he had lived in a cabin just a stone's throw from the boat launch ramp. His mother was the bridge attendant for many years back when the bridge had to be opened and closed by turning a large gear crank by hand.

Winston and I climbed into the skiff with Boaty, who brought the outboard motor to life, and we puttered back north toward Siesta Key and Sarasota looking for signs of mullet.

The first two spots Boaty tried netted only a half-dozen mullet, but the third one turned out to be the charm. Boaty cut the motor near the seawall of a small, rocky-bottomed bay, and we sat quietly on the water, watching mullet jump a few yards away. While Winston held the skiff in position with the

When Boaty Boatwright casts a net, he's sure to get a mess of mullet—just like the Calusa Indians did 400 years ago. Photograph by Winston Luzier.

poling oar, Boaty slipped into the waist-deep water with his cast net draped over his shoulder and noiselessly approached the school of fish. When he had gotten as close as he dared, he stood silent in the water and then made a quick twist and released the net. It fanned out perfectly to its full 8-foot radius just above the surface of the water. (If you throw your net too high in the air, the mullet can see it and escape.) The lead weights ringing the net's circumference splashed loudly as the net hit the water and sank to the bottom. Boaty quickly began pulling on the draw line, closing the net around a crowd of thrashing mullet. Then he began the "choking."

Grabbing mullet after mullet through the net mesh, Boaty inserted his fingers into the gill slots on each side of their bodies, and with his thumbs at the back of their heads, snapped down, breaking their necks. "That's mullet choking," Winston explained. "It accomplishes two things: It keeps the fish from escaping your net, and it also bleeds the fish, so you get a whiter, better-tasting fillet when you clean it."

By the time Boaty had shucked the mullet from his net, we had a pretty good-size pile of fish lying in the bottom of the skiff. "I think we can call it quits," Winston told him. "This is plenty enough to smoke today."

"One more throw," Boaty said, already getting his net in position and creeping away in the water. "That last one didn't scare them away at all. There's still a whole bunch of fish out here!"

Watching Boaty throwing his net and pulling it back to him loaded with mullet, I thought he could have been a Calusa Indian 400 years ago. The activity is basically the same now as it was back then and the goal too—to put a load of food on the table for an investment of very little sweat equity and time. Plus you're out on the water in the fresh air and sunshine, and it's fun.

I couldn't hold that reverie however. My gaze was drawn to the modern mansion just beyond the seawall 20 yards to our right, where a well-dressed man stood behind a two-story wall of plate glass talking on his cell phone.

● ● ● ● ●

We ended up with two large coolers full of mullet. It took a while to fillet them, and we were smoking mullet way into the evening. But none of that bothered Winston. He was in his element—he is a smoking man.

Smoked mullet, smoked roe—that's the only way he goes. Salt and pepper the fillets, soak them down with Tabasco sauce, and get them over the fire. He uses a smoker custom-made by his father from a 50-gallon steel drum. A hinged door at the base allows him to build and restoke the fire, metal rods run through the drum and hold a stack of three wire-mesh trays for the mullet, and a smokestack and damper are welded to the top. His father made his first models of this type smoker out of regular No. 10 aluminum garbage cans, but they just didn't hold enough mullet. And that wouldn't do because Winston smokes a lot of mullet.

He got a big kick out of relating an encounter he had with one of his neighbors.

"This neighborhood is a very desirable location." he told me, "A doctor bought the house behind me. He paid a pile of money for it, and the first thing he did was to start building a brick wall to separate his yard from mine. Well I was out here one Saturday smoking some mullet, and the smoke was drifting into his yard. He came to his wall, which was about shoulder high, and asked me if I did this often—meaning the smoker. Only every weekend, I told him. Man, it was hilarious. The following Monday he had a crew back out here and he took that wall up another three feet!"

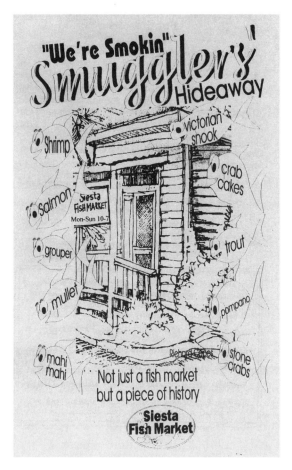

Locals and visitors alike rave about the smoked mullet and smoked mullet spread at this historic fish market.

SIESTA FISH MARKET

The Siesta Fish Market is the oldest continuously operating business on Siesta Key, one of the oldest and most upscale areas in Sarasota. When Guy Asbury bought the place in 1992, he knew he was buying a piece of Florida history. What he didn't know was that he was also buying into the biggest headache of his life.

Almost from the moment he took ownership Asbury has been embroiled in a battle with a gang of five "newly arrived neighbors," as described by the weekly *Pelican Press,* whose primary goal in life it seems is to shut the market down. These myopic citizens are of the "prominent" variety, and they have used their clout to spur the Sarasota City Commission to declare the market to be in violation of the city zoning code, thereby forcing it out of business. So far the commission members have obliged, and Guy Asbury finds himself in a lonely and nightmarish legal fight that, by his estimation, has already cost him over $200,000.

● ● ● ● ●

You won't find anything that is more "Old Florida" than the Siesta Fish Market. And you wouldn't find it at all (unless a local was bringing you) if there wasn't a modest but brightly colored sign on Higel Avenue with an arrow pointing down Garden Lane, which is little more than a short narrow trail running past Smuggler's Cove and the market before it turns into another narrow lane that runs you back north into the main drag on Siesta Key.

The market compound is virtually unchanged from the time it was established in 1932 by Ida and Lonnie Blount on four lots they bought for $25 each. There is the wood-frame fish house/market (modernized of course, but barely so) and two Cracker cabins that were built in 1923 and brought by barge from the mainland to their present site. Adjacent to the market is the screened-in smokehouse, with its blackened smoker, that the Blounts built in 1935 of a shell-and-mortar mixture known in these parts as coquina stone.

Lonnie Blount had been the dredge captain for Harry Higel, the man the present-day avenue is named after and the man who platted and dredged the key and made the canals. Lonnie was also occasionally the yacht captain for John Ringling, the wealthy and famous circus impresario. He was in his lifetime, it seems, a lot of "occasional" things.

Ida Blount, reportedly no less a colorful character than her husband, was in charge of the fish house, which processed all manner of fish and shellfish from the local bays. In addition she ran an oyster bar (oysters shucked on the premises) and sold lots and lots of smoked mullet. The place was very successful, and the clientele was not just your run-of-the-mill mulletheads. Even back in the days when the Blounts owned the market, the surrounding neighborhood was the high end of Siesta Key. All the big names of Sarasota, including John Ringling, had residences there and were customers. Eleanor Roosevelt, whose uncle had a house down the road, came in frequently when she was in town. Baseball great Ted Williams would drop by when his team was in training camp in Sarasota.

"Over the years it's been a bit of everything," says Guy Asbury," but mainly we processed mullet. Before the net ban in 1995, the gross of the business was seventy-five percent mullet and mullet roe and twenty-five percent retail fish. When the ban took effect the wholesale gross fell from about $750,000 a year to $250,000 gross. That was a damn hard hit, so in order to make up for the loss in gross wholesale, I put a few of these tables out here and dolled it up."

(The dolling up Asbury mentions was putting five white-plastic tables with canvas umbrellas in the leafy bowered yard, strewn with tropical flowering plants, between the market and the Cracker cabins.)

Asbury does admit that the fish market has had a checkered history since it passed out of the Blounts' hands. "Before I bought it there were seven convicted felons living here. Okay? They did import 'square grouper'—cocaine. I mean one guy is a habitual criminal. He's away for life now. Another guy is in prison for dealing a bunch of cocaine.

"It was the remnants of old pirates. That's what they really were down here. This road was unfit to walk down by a single woman at any time of day. That was just five years ago. Now when I bought the place, I walked around like *Walking Tall*. I mean I had a baseball bat—actually an ax handle, which I still have—and a .25 caliber pistol. I mean there was a hanging just down the lane, and there was a murder in the house across the way. All that was blamed on me, but it was just close! I inherited the reputation! Hell, all I got left now is stone crabbers, a few hand-toss mullet guys."

You'd think the "neighbors" would have been thankful for Asbury's presence after hearing that list of horrors, but instead

Tragically a few "newly arrived neighbors" have been trying to force Siesta Key's "oldest continuously operating business" to close. Photograph courtesy of Guy Asbury.

they complained about such things as him playing loud music and the disruption of the peace caused by the eighteen-wheel trucks delivering his fish. "First of all there have never been any eighteen-wheelers," Asbury says. "They couldn't make the turn to get in here. Second, if I sold one hundred pounds of fish a day, I'd be ecstatic! And how many eighteen-wheelers does it take to bring one hundred pounds of fish?"

As for the music I can testify from my visits to the market that I only heard classical playing on the sound system. On top of that the place doesn't even sell booze (though customers are allowed to bring their own), and it closes at 7 p.m.

"One of my problems is that I'm outspoken," Asbury says laughing from deep down in his near $6^1/_2$-foot frame. "I called them 'unctuous, bumptious, mendacious baboons.'"

I had to laugh myself, but Asbury's situation is anything but a laughing matter. He is mired down in and being pulled under by a system that should be protecting him and helping him to survive. (Not to mention he's going broke in the process.)

The Siesta Fish Market has been given a listing on The Heritage Trail, but that has been of no benefit. Asbury's attempts to have the market designated a historical site by the city were unsuccessful.

There is a Florida law, seemingly written specifically for the Siesta Fish Market, that states that no local authority "shall adopt any ordinance that declares any commercial or recreational fishing operation to be a nuisance solely because it is a commercial or recreational fishing operation, or any zoning ordinance that unreasonably forces the closure of any commercial or recreational fishing operation."

In a January 1998 ruling in one of Asbury's lawsuits, the court declared that his fish market was indeed covered by the law but that the city might have a "reasonable" cause to shut him down. In other words see you back in court—in eight or nine months—if you make it that long.

This is worse than a damn shame. It is a tragedy.

For if we lose the Siesta Fish Market, we lose not only a piece of history, we lose a restaurant that makes one of the best versions of smoked mullet I have ever eaten. It was without a doubt the spiciest, using a goodly amount of cayenne pepper, which, having lived in South Louisiana for sixteen years, suited my taste buds just fine. As for ambience the joint was at the top of the list.

AUTHOR'S NOTE: This story is Guy's version. It's the only version I needed to hear. I'm not an "objective" reporter, I'm a mullethead. Guy's enemies are the enemies of mulletheads everywhere. They not only don't care about destroying the past, they won't rest until they wipe out even the symbols of it. They are a despicable bunch.

At the time I had to surrender this manuscript to my publisher, the only hope for Asbury was his application for a historic designation from the State of Florida, which would supersede all actions of the city and keep him in business.

CODA

"Only a mullethead would move this boat," Michael Lathrop said when I met him at the Pasadena Beach marina.

He was talking about a 33-foot, twin-diesel powered Bertram Sportfish, a very expensive craft that he had just signed a contract to sell. And he was right—anyone with any sense would have left it just where it was until the new owner took possession. But he was compelled to take it out for a farewell cruise, and he had invited me to join him. Of course I had accepted.

We proceeded at a slow and pleasant—and thankfully— nondisastrous pace out into the Gulf, cruising past Mullet Key south to Egmont Key and then circling back. As we were coming out of the Gulf at idle speed through the pass to Ciega Bay, we passed a guy in a skintight wet suit and cap and goggles, furiously paddling a kayak against the strong Gulf waves.

"Did you see that?" Lathrop asked me.

"Yes. I did."

He was silent for a moment, and then he said, "That guy is not a mullethead."

He was right for the second time that afternoon, and pondering his comment, I had a sort of epiphany. What the kayaker was up to had too much of a purpose to it. It was not something a mullethead would be interested in. Mulletheads are more attuned to whimsy and serendipity.

Michael Lathrop, co-owner of Ted Peters Famous Smoked Fish and chief among mulletheads, understands that mullet—and mulletheads—"do it for the sheer joy of doing it." Photograph by Linda Swindle.

The defining characteristic of a mullethead, I realized that afternoon, is that they hear what the mullet hears just before it rockets out of the water and enjoys until the belly flop.

A RESTAURANT GUIDE FOR MULLETHEADS

I compiled the following list of restaurants and seafood houses as I drove along the Gulf Coast from Gulf Shores, Alabama, to Sarasota, Florida, stopping every time I saw the word "mullet," and making side trips when I was advised to do so. I cannot claim that this is a definitive list. I probably missed some places where you can eat mullet—but it was not for lack of trying.

Mikee's
Second Avenue East and
    First Street North
Gulf Shores, Alabama
334/948-6452
Fried mullet served on Tuesdays and Fridays.

Pink Pony Pub
At the public beach
Gulf Shores, Alabama
334/948-6371
Fried mullet served on Fridays.

Sea–n–Suds
405 East Beach Boulevard
Gulf Shores, Alabama
334/948-7894
Fried mullet served on Tuesdays and Fridays.

Doc's Seafood Shack
    & Oyster Bar
Intersection of Highway 180
    and Highway 161
Orange Beach, Alabama
334/981-6999
Fried mullet served on Tuesdays and Thursdays.

Perdido Cove Seafood
Restaurant
13141 Highway 98 (on
the Florida side of the
Lillian, Alabama, bridge)
Pensacola, Florida
850/455-9027

*Fried, broiled, grilled, and black-
ened mullet served every day.*

The Original Point Restaurant
14340 Innerarity Point Road
on Innerarity Point
Pensacola, Florida
904/492-3577

Fried mullet served every day.

Rusty's Restaurant & Lounge
10000 Sinton Drive (off Old
Gulf Beach Highway)
Pensacola, Florida
904/492-1657

*Home of the mullet backbone;
mullet served every day.*

The Oyster Bar
709 North Navy Boulevard
Pensacola, Florida
850/455-3925

*Fried mullet and broiled mullet
fillets served every day.*

Chet's Seafood Restaurant
"One Bite and You're
Hooked"
3708 Navy Boulevard
Pensacola, Florida
850/456-0165

*There is practically always a
line at this popular mullet
specialty place; fried and broiled
mullet fillets, mullet backbones,
and mullet fingers served on
Thursdays, Fridays, and
Saturdays, 11 a.m. to 9 p.m.*

The Original Doris's Restaurant
650 John Sims Parkway
Niceville, Florida
850/729-1636

*Fried mullet served on Thursday
nights and Fridays.*

The Boathouse Restaurant
"On Beautiful Boggy Bayou"
126 John Sims Parkway
Valparaiso, Florida
850/678-8839

*Call ahead—mullet is not served
every day at this converted "Old
Florida" house with a lovely deck
overlooking Boggy Bayou.*

Niceville Seafood
153 John Sims Parkway
Valparaiso, Florida
850/678-3949

Smoked mullet served to go.

Chapman's Seafood
  & Steak House
Highway 331 South
Freeport, Florida
850/835-2625

*Fried mullet served on a
regular basis.*

Harbor Docks Restaurant
538 Highway 98 East
Destin, Florida
850/837-7559

*They catch their own mullet
and serve an all-you-can-eat
fried mullet special seven days
a week.*

Esther's Soul Food
3127 East Business
  Highway 98
Springfield, Florida
904/763-1898

*Fried mullet served every day
at this African American-owned
restaurant.*

Linda's Restaurant
203 East Fourth Street
Port St. Joe, Florida
904/227-1109

*Fried mullet served usually
on Thursdays.*

Seafood-2-Go Retail Market
123A Water Street
Apalachicola, Florida
850/653-8044

*Fresh and smoked mullet
served to go.*

The Gibson Inn
Downtown on Highway 98
Apalachicola, Florida
904/653-2191

*Mullet served on an irregular
basis, but this beautifully
restored historic hotel is
worth a stop all by itself.*

Sharon's Place Restaurant &
  Seafood Market
Highway 98 (just east
  of Apalachicola)
Eastpoint, Florida
904/670-8646

*Fried mullet served when it's
available.*

Julia Mae's
"World Famous"
Highway 98
Carrabelle, Florida
904/697-3791

*Fried mullet served when it's
available.*

The Oaks Motel Restaurant
Highway 98 at the bridge
Panacea, Florida
850/984-5370

*Fried mullet and mullet fillets
served on a regular basis.*

Posey's Seafood & Steak
   Restaurant
Highway 98 "Beyond the
   Bay" (across the street
   from Metcalf Seafood)
Panacea, Florida
904/984-5799

*For a mullet place, Posey's is
pretty upscale but also very
down-home—and a hit with
the locals, who are no strangers
to good mullet. Fried mullet
served on a regular basis;
baked, broiled, and blackened
mullet sometimes available.*

Metcalf Seafood
Highway 98 (across from
   Posey's Seafood & Steak
   Restaurant)
Panacea, Florida
904/984-0010

Smoked mullet served to go.

Coastal Restaurant
Highway 98 "In the
   Heart of Panacea"
Panacea, Florida
904/984-2933

*This no-frills last bastion of
"all-you-can-eat" fried mullet
is open every day except
Tuesdays and Wednesdays.
(I never passed this place
without stopping to eat.)*

D. L. Thomas Seafood
Highway 98
Panacea, Florida
904/984-5391

Smoked mullet served to go.

Posey's Oyster Bar
Highway 98
St. Marks, Florida
850/925-6172

This place sits right on St. Marks River off Highway 98, and you can watch mullet being cleaned on the back deck. It's one of my Top Three choices for the best smoked mullet.

Ouzts' Oyster Bar and
    Canoe Rental
Highway 98 East at
    St. Marks River Bridge
Newport, Florida
850/925-6448

"Eat mo' mullet" is the motto of this very funky little place. (When I asked for directions to the men's room, a regular told me, "Out the front door and around the corner to your right, or the first palm tree that looks familiar.") Smoked mullet and beer served.

Pouncey's Restaurant
2186 South Byron Butler
    Parkway (Highway 19)
Perry, Florida
904/584-9942

Fried mullet served on a regular basis; baked and broiled mullet sometimes available.

Roy's Restaurant
Junction of Highways 51 and 361
Steinhatchee, Florida
352/498-5000

Fried mullet served when it's available.

Johnson & Allen's Seafood
State Road 24
Cedar Key, Florida
904/543-5447

Smoked mullet and Mrs. Johnson's "famous" and delicious smoked mullet spread served to go.

Cooke's Oysters & Seafood
12811 State Road 24
Cedar Key, Florida
352/543-5334

Smoked mullet, smoked mullet spread, and fresh mullet roe (in season) served.

Captain's Table Restaurant/
    Captain's Quarters Lounge
222 Dock Street
Cedar Key, Florida
352/543-5441

Fried and broiled mullet served.

Brown Pelican Restaurant
Dock Street
Cedar Key, Florida
352/543-5428

*Fried and broiled mullet
and smoked mullet spread
served.*

Pat's Red Luck Cafe
Dock Street
Cedar Key, Florida
352/543-6840

*Fried mullet served on an
irregular basis—but always
with lima beans.*

Seabreeze on the Dock
Dock Street
Cedar Key, Florida
352/543-5738

*Mullet "mealed and fried
which has bones" served
when it's available.*

John's One Stop Bar-B-Q
Yulee Road
Homosassa, Florida
352/628-4929

*Fried mullet sandwiches and
dinners served.*

Yulee Cafe
10605 Yulee Road
Homosassa, Florida
352/628-7177

Fried mullet served.

Maggie Mae's BBQ
On the river in "historic
    downtown Homosassa"
Homosassa, Florida
(no telephone at this place)

Smoked mullet served.

The Mullet Hut
    (a caboose-like trailer)
Sunnybrook Shopping Plaza
    parking lot on Highway 19
Homosassa, Florida
(no telephone at this place)

*Very good smoked mullet and a
Cajun-flavored smoked mullet
spread (like a dip, but delicious
nonetheless) served on Fridays,
Saturdays, and Sundays.*

The Mullet Boat
701 North Pinellas Avenue
    (Alternate Highway 19)
Tarpon Springs, Florida
904/937-7229

*Smoked mullet and smoked
mullet spread served.*

Red Roe Smokehouse
  Restaurant
"Ol' Florida Dining on
  Banana Creek"
303 Orange Street
Ozona, Florida
813/784-0535

*Fresh, fried, and smoked
mullet served.*

J. Matassini & Sons Fish
  Co., Inc.
2008 Garcia Avenue
Tampa, Florida
813/229-0829

*The oldest fish house in Tampa;
serves smoked mullet to go.*

Ted Peters Famous
  Smoked Fish
1350 Pasadena Avenue
Pasadena Beach, Florida
813/381-7931

*Mullethead Heaven! Believe me!
At the top of my Top Three list.
Serves the definitive smoked
mullet (dinners and by the
pound to go) and the definitive
smoked mullet spread (like ham
salad only mullet instead of ham).*

The Star Fish Company
12306 46th Avenue West
Cortez, Florida
941/794-1243

*This fresh seafood market and
cafe right on the water in this
historic fishing village serves
Cortez-style smoked and fried
mullet and fresh mullet roe
(in season).*

Siesta Fish Market
221 Garden Lane
Sarasota, Florida
941/349-2602

*Established in 1932, they
know what they're doing with
smoked mullet. One of my
Top Three for the best of this
delicacy.*

Photograph by UPI/Corbis-Bettmann.

MULLET RECIPES

James Campbell's Basic Fried Mullet

"There are different ways to do it, but there's one simple way. You peel the mullet, clean him good, milk him, salt and pepper him, and then you fry him. That's not real complicated, but some people can screw that up."

T. H. Lovell's Fried Mullet

Mullet	Cornmeal
Salt	Oil for deep-frying
Pepper	

Wash cleaned fresh fish. Salt and pepper fish generously, and roll in cornmeal.

Fry in deep, hot (350°) oil, turning if necessary, for 3 to 5 minutes or until fish flakes easily when tested with a fork. Fish will be golden brown. Drain on absorbent paper.

Fish-Frying Pointers: Use a large, deep pan to avoid crowding fish. Turn fish once when crisp and golden. For fillets, brown skin side last. After frying, drain fish immediately on paper towels to remove excess fat.

Ann Spence's Smoked Mullet

Butter
Dry mustard
Mullet
Lemon juice
Olive oil
Worcestershire sauce

Charcoal
Green hickory
Bay leaves
Sassafras roots
Thyme

Make a sauce of butter and dry mustard.

Marinate fish in lemon juice, olive oil, and Worcestershire sauce.

Smoke marinated fish over charcoal and green hickory, basting often with butter-mustard sauce. Halfway through cooking time, place bay leaves, sassafras roots, and thyme under fish; continue smoking until fish flakes easily when tested with a fork.

Boggy Bayou Smoked Mullet Spread

1½ pounds smoked mullet
2 teaspoons minced onions
2 teaspoons finely chopped celery
1 clove garlic, minced
2 tablespoons finely chopped sweet pickle
1¼ cups mayonnaise
1 tablespoon mustard
Dash Worcestershire sauce
2 tablespoons chopped parsley

Remove skin and bones from smoked fish, and flake well. Add remaining ingredients and mix well. Chill at least one hour.

Makes approximately 3½ cups.

Capt. William Frank Davis's "Charcoaled" Mullet

Mullet fillets
Lemons, cut in half
Salt
Pepper

Paprika
Bacon
1/8-inch-thick slices onion
Lemon wedges

Make a shallow "pan" of heavy aluminum foil.

Lay fish in single layer in pan. Squeeze lemon halves over fish, generously covering fish with juice. Season with salt, pepper, and paprika. Place two pieces of bacon on top of each fillet. Top with 1/8-inch slices of onion.

Cook on a charcoal grill with the top down until fish and onion are done, approximately 45 minutes. Serve with lemon wedges.

Gulf Fish Salad

2 1/2 cups cooked, flaked mullet
2 cups cold cooked rice
1 cup chopped celery
1/2 cup chopped parsley
1/4 cup sliced pitted ripe olives
1/2 cup mayonnaise or salad dressing
2 tablespoons French dressing
2 tablespoons lemon juice
1 teaspoon curry powder
Salad greens

Combine flaked fish, rice, celery, parsley, and olives. Combine mayonnaise, French dressing, lemon juice, and curry powder. Mix thoroughly and add to fish mixture; toss lightly and chill.

Serve on salad greens.

Makes 6 servings.

Mrs. Leonard E. Destin's Mullet Chowder

3½ pounds skinned and boned mullet fillets
½ cup chopped salt pork
2 medium onions, chopped
1 cup chopped celery stalks and leaves
3 cloves garlic, chopped
1 small green pepper, chopped
1 large can tomatoes
1 can tomato paste
2 tablespoons Worcestershire sauce
½ teaspoon liquid hot pepper sauce
1 tablespoon salt
1 teaspoon black pepper
2 cups boiling water
8 white potatoes, cut into chunks
2 large carrots, sliced

Cut fish into chunks.

In a large Dutch oven, fry salt pork until light brown. Add chopped onions, and cook until done. Add chopped celery, garlic, and green pepper, and cook for 5 minutes. Add tomatoes, tomato paste, Worcestershire sauce, hot pepper sauce, salt, and pepper. Cook 10 minutes.

Add 2 cups boiling water, potatoes, and carrots; cook until potatoes are nearly done.

Add fish and simmer until fish flakes easily when tested with a fork.

Makes 6 generous servings.

Buttermilk Fried Mullet With Lemon Relish

2 pounds skinless mullet fillets　2 teaspoons salt
I cup buttermilk　　　　　　　　Oil for deep-frying
I cup biscuit mix　　　　　　　　Lemon Relish

Cut fish into serving-size portions, and place in a single layer in a shallow dish. Pour buttermilk over fish, and let stand for 30 minutes, turning once.

Combine biscuit mix and salt. Remove fish from buttermilk, and coat with biscuit mix.

Place fish in a single layer in frying basket. Deep-fry in hot (350°) oil for 3 to 5 minutes or until fish is brown and flakes easily when tested with a fork. Drain on absorbent paper.

Serve with Lemon Relish.

Makes 6 servings.

Lemon Relish:

$1/2$ cup sour cream
$1/4$ cup crushed pineapple, drained
2 tablespoons finely chopped green pepper
I tablespoon finely chopped onion
I tablespoon light brown sugar
$1^{1}/2$ teaspoons grated lemon peel
$1/4$ teaspoon dry mustard
$1/4$ teaspoon celery salt
$1/8$ teaspoon ground cloves

Combine all ingredients; mix well and chill.

Makes approximately 1 cup.

Alan Frederiksen's *Ceviche du Mulet*

Skinless mullet fillets, cut into chunks
Fresh lime juice
Vidalia onions, chopped

Submerge chunks of raw fish under lime juice until "cooked."
Serve with chopped sweet Vidalia onions.

Alan Frederiksen's Pickled Mullet

Mix together a "good grade of pickling spices, wine and/or
vinegar, and a tablespoon of sugar to lessen acidity." Pour
pickling juices into Mason jars or a stone crock.

Cut "raw mullet fillets into strips, skin remaining as in herring
roll-mops, and place" in the pickling juices. Let the fish steep
"in the ferment a moon's length to mature."

Note: "Some folks lightly steam the fish strips before placing in
pickling juices. The skin of the mullet is chewier than herring;
it may be removed prior to serving."

Reggie Smith's Spicy Canned Mullet

Cut deboned mullet fillets into chunks, and pack into canning
jars.

Add jalapeno pepper cut in half (or more to your taste).

Process jars in pressure cooker (fish will make it's own juice).

Let canned fish sit as long as you can stand it before eating.

FOR MORE ABOUT MULLET

Barrister, B. B. and Jack C. Nichols. *Up, Down, In & Around Boggy Bayou*. Crestview, Fla.: Walk-a-bout Enterprises Inc., 1995.

Frederiksen, Alan. *Man & Mullet: An Elegy for a Lost Way of Life*. Homosassa, Fla.: Green Key Press, 1995.

_____. *Red Roe Run*. Homosassa, Fla.: Green Key Press, 1983.

Greene, Ed. *Fishing A Cast Net: Step by Step Instructions*. Tallahassee, Fla.: Greene Publications, 1989.

Isusi, Jose Maria Busca. *Traditional Basque Cooking*. Reno, Nev.: University of Nevada Press, 1987.

Josephy, Alvin M., Jr. *500 Nations: An Illustrated History of North American Indians*. New York: Alfred A. Knopf, 1994.

Kent, Richard. "Mullet Mania," *Tampa Bay Life* (November 1988).

McClane, A. J. *Encyclopedia of Fish Cookery*, New York: Holt, Rinehart and Winston, 1977.

_____, ed. *McClane's New Standard Fishing Encyclopedia and International Angling Guide*, rev. ed. New York: Holt, Rinehart and Winston, 1974.

Northwest Florida Water Management District. *Historical Remembrances of Choctawhatchee Bay, Northwest Florida,* Water Resources Special Report 85-2, December 1985.

Wood, Ian, ed. *The Dorling Kindersley Encyclopedia of Fishing.* New York: DK Publishing, 1994.